A Taoist Miscellany

Compiled by Yuan Guang
Translated by Cheng Yu

Foreign Languages Press Beijing

First Edition 1999

Managing Editor: Cheng Yu

Home Page:
http://www.flp.com.cn
E-mail Addresses:
info@flp.com.cn
sales@flp.com.cn

ISBN 7-119-02163-X

Published by Foreign Languages Press
24 Baiwanzhuang Road, Beijing 100037, China

Printed by Beijing Foreign Languages Printing House
19 Chegongzhuang Xilu, Beijing 100044, China

Distributed by China International Book Trading Corporation
35 Chegongzhuang Xilu, Beijing 100044, China
P.O. Box 399, Beijing, China

Printed in the People's Republic of China

CONTENTS

INTRODUCTION

Taoism, Confucianism and Buddhism are regarded as the three intellectual pillars of traditional Chinese culture. Taoism, which emphasizes doing nothing (non-action) and letting things take their own course, has been especially influential in the history of Chinese culture and thought.

Taoism followed a unique process of development. During the Qin (221-206 B.C.) and Han (206 B.C.-A.D. 220) dynasties, it was known as the "study of Huang and Lao." Huang, or Huangdi, was the mythical ancestor of the Chinese nation, and Lao, or Lao Zi, was the purported author of the *Tao Te Ching*—also known as *The Book of Lao Zi*, the representative classic of Taoism. *The Book of Lao Zi* was written in the late Spring and Autumn Period (770-476 B.C.); some chapters of the book may have been written during the Warring States Period (475-221 B.C.).

Sima Tan, father of the Western Han Dynasty (206 B.C.-A.D. 24) historian Sima Qian, said, "Taoism helps one to concentrate the mind, act unobtrusively and care for all things on earth. As a way to self-cultivation, it follows the nature of Yin and Yang (the ultimate positive and negative, and male and female essences in Nature), takes up the strong points of Confucianism and Mohism, absorbs the essentials of Logicianism and Legalism, adapts to the changes of the times, follows the nature of everything and can be used everywhere. It is easy to practice, as its precepts are simple, and it can help people accomplish much with little effort." As it absorbed the strong points of all the major schools of thought and stressed self-cultivation as the way to rule the world, Taoism received great attention from the imperial court in the early years of the Western Han, when the country was just recovering from long years of war.

Taoism embodies knowledge of Nature, social development, human relationships and other rich and subtle wisdom of the ancient Chinese people. Tao literally means "the way." It includes the way of Nature, the way of all things on earth, the way of social changes, the way of running a country, the way of self-cultivation and managing a family, even the way of "living a long life with good eyes and ears," which encapsulates the ideal of the ancestors of the Chinese people as regards their approach to life.

The ancient Chinese medical and health-preservation techniques almost all drew their inspiration from Taoism, and works appeared expounding on ways of self-cultivation and long life based on Lao Zi's teachings. Eventually, Taoism was combined with religion, and Lao Zi was elevated to the status of an immortal.

Unlike Confucianism and Buddhism, the hallmark of the Taoist school of philosophy is its eclecticism; its adherents have included many learned thinkers, magicians, doctors, pharmacists and alchemists. And, as an indigenous way of thought, Taoism is uniquely Chinese in its contents and forms. Many stories from the treasure trove of Taoist lore have pure and fresh artistic concepts, focusing on the ideas of "governing by doing nothing" and "letting things take their own course."

The stories in this book reflect the vast range of Taoist thought, which at the same time contains ideas culled from virtually all the other schools of ancient Chinese philosophy and religion. Drawing on the rich corpus of classical Taoist literature, these pithy stories embody the mysterious wisdom of the "Way," which stimulates the reader's imagination while at the same time amusing and diverting him or her.

1. The Calabash and the Ointment for Chapped Hands

Hui Zi (Hui Tzu) (c. 370-310 B.C.), prime minister of King Hui of the State of Liang, once said to Zhuang Zi (Chuang Tzu): "My master, the king, sent me some calabash seeds. I planted them and they bore a fruit as big as a five-bushel measure. I tried to use it as a bowl for holding water, but it was not solid enough for the purpose. So I cut the calabash in two and tried to make two ladles out of it, but each of them was far too big for the purpose. Thereupon, because of their uselessness, I smashed them to pieces."

"Sir," said Zhuang Zi, "it is clear that you do not know how to make all things serve their proper purpose. Now, there was once a man of the State of Song who had a secret recipe for ointment for chapped hands. From generation to generation, his family had made the bleaching and dyeing of silk their occupation, and the ointment helped them to do this. A stranger heard of the ointment, and offered the man 100 ounces of gold for the recipe. The family gathered to consider this proposal. 'We have,' said they, 'been bleaching and dyeing silk for generations, and we never earned more than a pittance. Now all at once we can earn 100 ounces of gold simply by disclosing the recipe for the ointment we have been using. Let us not hesitate to sell it.' And so the stranger obtained the recipe. At the time, the State of Wu was at war with the State of Yue, during which many Wu soldiers could not fight with weapons because they had chapped hands in the cold weather. Having heard of this, the man from Song went straight to the king of the State of Wu and made him a present of the recipe. Later, the king of Wu gave the stranger the command of his fleet. When the Wu fleet crashed that of Yue, the stranger was rewarded with a fief and a title. Thus, while the efficiency of the ointment to cure chapped hands was the same whether it was used by the silk workers or by the stranger, in the former case it only served to help them perform a menial task, while in the latter case it brought a man fame and wealth. This was because they used it differently.

Now you, sir, had a five-bushel calabash; why did you not make of it a large bottle gourd, by means of which you could float in rivers and lakes? Instead of this, you were piqued that it was useless for holding anything. It seems that your mind is rather woolly."

Hui Zi said to Zhuang Zi: "I have a large tree, which people call the ailanthus, outside my house. Its trunk is so irregular and knotty that a carpenter cannot apply his line to it. Its small branches are so twisted that the square and compasses cannot be used on them. It stands by the roadside, but no carpenter takes cognizance of it. They all think, it seems, that the tree is useless despite its large size."

Zhuang Zi said, "Have you not seen a wild cat or a weasel? It lies, crouching down, in wait for its prey. East and west it leaps about, avoiding neither what is high nor what is low. At last it is caught in a trap or dies in a net. Again, there is the yak, which is as large as a cloud which crosses the sky. But it cannot catch mice. Now you have a large tree and fret about its uselessness. Why do you not plant it in the domain of nonexistence, in a wide and barren wilderness? By its side you may wander in non-action; under it you may sleep in happiness. Neither bill nor ax would shorten its term of existence. Though of no use to others, it would not cause worry to you either."

"Carefree Wanderings," *The Inner Chapters of Zhuang Zi*

Note: *Hui Zi (c.370-310 B.C.) and Zhuang Zi (c. 369-286 B.C.) were friends as well as adversaries in disputation. Hui Zi uses the analogy of the big calabash to criticize Zhuang Zi's ideas as wide-ranging and impractical. Zhuang Zi, on the other hand, uses the analogy of the ointment to explain that everything has its strong and weak points; whether something is big or small, it can be either useful or useless, depending upon the use it is put to.*

2. Carving Up an Ox as Skillfully as a Master Butcher

The personal cook of King Hui of Liang (400-319 B.C., reigned 369-319 B.C.) had a marvelously skillful way of carving up an ox. Every blow of his hand, every heave of his shoulder, every tread of his foot, every thrust of his knee, every sound of the rending flesh, and every note of the strokes of the cleaver were as graceful as music and dance. In the twinkling of an eye, a whole ox would be perfectly dismembered.

"How admirable," the king once cried, upon seeing this, "your consummate art! How did you achieve it?"

The cook laid down his cleaver and replied, "What your servant follows is the Tao, which is beyond mere art. When I first began to cut up oxen, I saw them as huge, whole animals and didn't know how and where to begin. Three years later, I had come to know the exact location of every part of their bodies—their bones, flesh, sinews, viscera, etc. I saw them no longer as whole animals. Now, I work with my mind, and not with my eyes. The functions of my senses stop; my spirit dominates. Following the natural veins, my cleaver slips through the great cavities and slides through the great openings, taking advantage of what is already there. I do not attempt the central veins and their branches, or the connectives between flesh and bone, not to mention the great bones!

"A good cook changes his cleaver once a year, because he cuts. An ordinary cook changes his cleaver once a month, because he hacks. Now my cleaver has been in use for 19 years. It has cut up one thousand oxen, yet its edge is still as sharp as if it had just come from the whetstone. At the joints there are always interstices, and the edge of the cleaver is without thickness. If I insert that which is without thickness into an interstice, there is certainly plenty of room for it to move along. Nevertheless, when I come to a complicated joint, I fix my eyes on it. I move slowly. Then, with a very gentle movement of my cleaver, the part is quickly separated and yields itself into my hand. I look around, with an air of triumph and satisfaction. Then I wipe my cleaver and put it back in its sheath."

"Excellent!" said the king. "From a lowly cook, I have actually learned the way to cultivate life."

"The Fundamentals of the Cultivation of Life," *The Inner Chapters of Zhuang Zi*

Note: *Everything, no matter how complex, has its own law. If you study profoundly and grasp the nature of a matter it is* *easy to deal with. Through this anecdote, Zhuang Zi teaches that in a complicated society, people must act like the cook in order to survive and thrive. He who can make use of his skill and experience to solve problems easily, as the cook does, will be free from harm, just like the cook's knife.*

3. The Mantis and the Chariot

Qu Boyu was a sage of the State of Wei. Yan He from the State of Lu was invited to be the tutor of the heir apparent to the ruler of Wei, Duke Ling (534-493 B.C.). Accordingly, Yan He consulted Qu Boyu, saying,

"Here is a man whose disposition is naturally of a low order. If I allow him to proceed without principle, it will be at the peril of our state. If I insist on his proceeding according to principle, it will be at the peril of my own person. He has just enough wit to see the faults of others, but not his own. What am I to do in such a case?"

"A good question, indeed," replied Qu Boyu. "You must be careful and begin with self-reformation. For your external bearing, there is nothing better than adaptation and conformity. For your inner mind, there is nothing better than peace and harmony. Yet in these there are two points to guard against: You must not let the external adaptation penetrate within, nor the inner harmony manifest itself without. In the former case, you will fall, you will ruin yourself, you will collapse, you will tumble; in the latter case, you will gain an evil

reputation and bring disaster on yourself. If the son of the duke should act as if he were a child, you also should act as if you were a child. If he should cast aside all differences, you should do the same. If he should cast aside all distinctions, you also should do the same. Then you can lead him to innocence."

After being lost in thought for a while, Qu Boyu continued, "Do you not know the story of the mantis? In its rage it stretches out its feelers to arrest the progress of an oncoming carriage, without knowing that it is not qualified to do so; it thinks it has superb ability. In attempting what is impossible, it only courts its own doom. Be on your guard. Be careful. If you always show your excellence to others and thus offend them, probably you yourself will be in danger. Do you not know how a keeper of tigers handles them? He does not venture to give them living animals as food, for fear of exciting their fury when killing them. He does not venture to give them whole animals as food, for fear of exciting their fury when rending them. He knows when the tigers are hungry and when they are sated; he understands the reasons for their being angry. The tigers are a different species from man, yet they try to please their keeper. That is because he adapts himself to them. There are some people who act in conflict with the nature of the tigers. These the tigers will kill if they have the opportunity.

Those who are fond of horses collect the dung and urine of the horses in baskets and jars. Sometimes mosquitoes and gadflies light on a horse. Then, in order to brush them off, the groom strikes the horse. The result is that the horse breaks the bit and hurts the groom's head and chest. The groom intends to do something good, but in the end, what he intends to do goes away. Ought we not then to be cautious?"

"The Human World," *The Inner Chapters of Zhuang Zi.*

Note: *This story points out that people who are overconfident are heading for disaster. Zhuang Zi stresses the supreme importance of following Nature. Even a fierce tiger can be rendered docile if you deal with it in conformity with its nature, and the complacent horse will rear up if its nature is contravened.*

4. The Carpenter's Dream

A master carpenter on his way to the State of Qi came to a place called Qu Yuan. There he saw a big oak tree, which was worshipped by the local people as the repository of the god of that place. It was so large that many oxen standing behind it could not be seen. It measured 100 spans around, and towered for 80 cubits on a hill before it threw out any branches. Of the branches, there were a dozen or so, from each of which a whole boat could be hollowed out. People came to see it in crowds, so that the surrounding area was just like a busy market place. But the master carpenter hardly deigned to give it a glance, but passed it by without stopping. His apprentices, however, looked at it till their eyes were tired. Then they ran up to their master, and said to him:

"Since we started to follow you with our tools, we have never seen timber as good as that. Why, sir, did you not stop to look at it? Instead, you walked straight past it!"

"Enough!" said their master, with a smile: "That wood is useless. A boat made from it would sink; a coffin would quickly rot, an article of furniture would soon fall to pieces, a pillar would be riddled with insects. It is useless and good for nothing. That is why it has attained to so great an age."

That night, the sacred tree appeared to the master carpenter in a dream, saying, "With what other trees would you compare me? Would you compare me with the useful trees? There are hawthorns, pear trees, orange trees, pomelo trees and others. The fruits are knocked down when they are ripe, and the trees are abused. The large branches are broken, and the smaller ones torn off. The life of these plants is one of suffering, because of their productive ability. They, therefore, cannot complete their natural term of existence, but come to a premature end in the middle of their time, and bring upon themselves destructive treatment from society. It is so with all things. Over a long period of time I learned to be useless. There were several occasions on which I was nearly destroyed. Now I have succeeded in being useless, which is of the greatest use to me; if I were useful, could I have become so great? Moreover, you and I are both things; how can one thing pass judgment upon another? You are also a useless man and near death. How can you understand a useless tree?"

When the master carpenter awoke, he told his apprentices about the dream. "But if its ambition is to be useless, why does it serve as the repository of the local god?" asked the apprentices.

"Enough of your foolish chatter!" the master carpenter replied. "The tree just pretends to be the repository of the local god. By so doing it can protect itself from injury by those who do not know that it is useless. If it were not thought to be the repository of the god, it would be in danger of being cut down. Moreover, what this tree does is different from what ordinary trees do. Therefore, to praise it from the viewpoint of conventional morality is to be wide of the mark.

"The Human World," *The Inner Chapters of Zhuang Zi*

Note: *This fable presents the idea of the "use of useless." It is considered that being useful is harmful and being useless is lucky. The author points out the useful things suffer while useless things are left in peace.*

5. The Forge and Nature

Zi Si, Zi Yu, Zi Li and Zi Lai were friends. They made the following vow: "Whosoever can make nothing the head of his existence, life its backbone and death its tail; whosoever knows that life and death, existence and nonexistence, are one—that man shall be our friend."

Not long after, Zi Lai fell ill, and lay gasping at the point of death, while his wife wept around him. Zi Li went to see him, and said to his friend's wife: "Go, hush, get out of the way. Do not disturb the natural evolution." Then, leaning against the door, he said to Zi Lai:

"Great is Nature! What will she make of you? Will she make you into the liver of a rat? Will she make you into the leg of an insect?"

"Wherever a parent tells a child to go, " replied Zi Lai, "east, west , south, or north, the child simply follows the command. Nature—Yin and Yang—is no other than a human being's parent. If she bid me die quickly, and I demur, then I am obstinate and rebellious; she does no wrong. Man does wrong because he does not know the Tao of Nature. The universe carries me in my body, makes me toil through my life, gives me repose in old age, and rests me in death. What makes my life good makes my death good also. Imagine the great foundryman Mo Xie, casting metal in his forge. If the metal should leap up and say: 'I must be made into a sword!' the great foundryman would certainly regard it as impertinent. Now, if I in my original essence were to say to the maker of all things: 'I must be a man, I must be a man!' the Maker would certainly regard me as impertinent. If we take the universe as a great melting pot, and Nature as a great foundryman, what place is it not right for us to go? Calmly we die; quietly we live."

Then Zi Lai died.

"The Great Teacher," *The Inner Chapters of Zhuang Zi*

Note: *He who desires to cultivate himself in the proper way must know how to face both life and death. This story indicates that only he who surrenders to Nature in both living and dying can know the Tao of Nature.*

6. Fish and Water, Man and the Tao

Zi Sang Hu, Meng Zi Fan, and Zi Qin Zhang were friends. Originally they said to each other: "Who can associate in non-association, and cooperate in non-cooperation? Who can mount to Heaven and roam through the clouds, disporting in the infinite and become oblivious of existence, forever and ever without end?" The three men looked at each other and smiled, silently agreed one with another, and thus became friends.

Several years later, Zi Sang Hu died. Before he was buried, Confucius heard of the event, and sent his disciple Zi Gong to represent him at the mourning rites. Zi Gong found that one of the friends had composed a song, and the other was playing on the lute. They were singing in unison:

"Alas! Sang Hu! Sang Hu! You have returned to the real, but we remain here as men. Alas!"

The two men looked at each other and laughed.

Puzzled, Zi Gong asked, "Gentlemen, may I venture to ask whether it is decorous to sing in the presence of the deceased?"

The other two exclaimed, "What does this man

know about the idea of decorum?"

Zi Gong went back and reported this to Confucius, asking him, "What sort of men are those? They have no culture and consider their bodies as external to themselves. They sing in the presence of the deceased, without a change of countenance. I do not know what to call them."

"They travel outside the human world, " said Confucius, "while both you and I travel within it. There is no common ground for these two ways; I was wrong in sending you there to mourn. They are the unity of the universe. They consider life as an appendage attached to them, an excrescence annexed to them. They consider death as a separation of the appendage, and a dispersion of the excrescence. With these views, how can they be aware of the superiority of life and the inferiority of death? They consider their bodies as compositions of different borrowed elements. They regard them merely as temporary lodgings. They forget their livers and gall bladders, and ignore their ears and eyes. They end and they begin without knowing either the beginning or the end. Unconsciously, they stroll beyond the sordid world and wander in the realm of non-action. How can they foolishly trouble themselves with conventionalities simply for the sake of ordinary people?"

"If such is the case, " said Zi Gong, "why should you, Master, stick to the conventionalities?"

"I am nature's condemned one," said Confucius.

"However, that is what we have in common."

"May I venture to ask you to give a further explanation?" asked Zi Gong.

"Fishes thrive in water; men thrive in the Tao," said Confucius. "Enjoying water, the fishes cleave to the pools, and their nourishment is thus adequate. Enjoying the Tao, men do nothing and their lives are thus self-sufficient. Hence it is said, 'Fishes forget one another in rivers and lakes; men forget one another in the Tao.' "

"Aren't such people abnormal men?" asked Zi Gong.

"The abnormal man is abnormal to man but is normal to nature," said Confucius. "Therefore, it is said, 'The inferior man for nature is a superior man among men; the superior man for nature is an inferior man among men."

"The Great Teacher," *The Inner Chapters of Zhuang Zi*

Note: *This fable compares fish and water with men and the Tao. The author regards life and death as part of a unified process which circles over and over again, without beginning or end. He who wishes to follow the way of nature must be happy in doing nothing.*

7. Hu Zi Practices Physiognomy

In the State of Zheng there was a renowned wizard named Ji Xian. He knew all about men's births and deaths, gains and losses, misfortunes and joys—predicting the year, the month, and the day of any event with supernatural accuracy. The people of Zheng used to flee at his approach for fear of hearing unpleasant predictions from him. Lie Zi (a disciple of Hu Zi) went to see the wizard and was fascinated. On his return, he said to Hu Zi, "I used to consider your doctrine, Master, as perfect. Now I know something more perfect still."

"So far I have taught you but the literature of my doctrine," smiled Hu Zi, "but not its essence. Do you think that you are in possession of it? Without cocks in your poultry yard, what sort of eggs would the hens lay? You displayed your doctrine to the world in order to get credit. That is the reason why this man can interpret your physiognomy. Bring to me this sorcerer of yours, pray."

The next day, Lie Zi took Ji Xian to see Hu Zi, and when they came out, Ji Xian said, "Alas! your master is a dead man! He will not live—not for ten days more!

I saw something strange about him. He looked like wet ashes."

Lie Zi went back in, where he wept till the front of his jacket was wet with tears. Then he told Hu Zi what the wizard had said. Hu Zi simply smiled and said: "I showed myself to him in the form of earth. I was naturally immovable like a mountain, though I made no artificial attempt to be immovable. He probably saw me with my natural functions closed up. Try to bring him again."

The next day, accordingly, Lie Zi brought the wizard again to see Hu Zi. When they went out, the wizard said, "It is fortunate for your master that he met me. He is better. He is full of life. I see that the closing up of his natural functions was only temporary."

Lie Zi told Hu Zi what Ji Xian had said. Hu Zi said, "I showed myself to him in the form of heaven. Fame and real gain do not enter my mind. My natural functions spring forth from the depth of my being. He probably saw me with my natural functions in full activity. Try to bring him again."

The next day Lie Zi again brought the wizard to see Hu Zi. When they went out, the wizard said, "Your master is never the same. I cannot understand his physiognomy. Wait until he has become normal, and then I will examine him again."

Hu Zi told Lie Zi: "I showed myself to him in the great harmony in which nothing is superior to anything. He probably saw the balance of my natural functions. Where the water whirls about from the swishing of a dugong, there is a whirlpool; where it does so from the checking of its flow, there is a whirlpool; where it does so from the onward rushing of its flow, there is a whirlpool. There are nine kinds of whirlpools, with different names. I have only mentioned three of them. Try to bring him again."

The next day Lie Zi again came with the wizard to see Hu Zi. But even before he had seated himself properly, the wizard lost control of himself and ran away. Hu Zi said, "Bring him back!" Lie Zi tried, but could not catch him.

Hu Zi said, "I showed myself to him, with change but without losing the essential. I flexibly followed him with emptiness. I do not know who is who or what is what. In accordance with things, I change; in accordance with things, I flow. That is why he ran away."

Upon hearing this, Lie Zi was convinced that he had not yet acquired any real learning. He returned to his house, and for three years he did not go out. He cooked for his wife and fed his pigs. He discarded the artificial and reverted to the natural. He stood in the world like a clod of earth. Amidst confusion and disturbance, he remained within the One to the last.

"The Philosopher-King," *The Inner Chapters of Zhuang Zi*

Note: *Ji Xian glorified himself through his ability to predict life and death, but he failed before Hu Zi. That is, in fact, the failure of prediction (useful), whereas non-prediction (useless) can never fail. This story describes the mystery of the Tao. Only by doing nothing, can people return to their original nature.*

8. The Yellow Emperor Asks About the Tao

Four thousand or five thousand years ago, the Yellow Emperor had been the master of the world for 19 years: The whole world followed his edicts. Then he heard that Guang Cheng Zi was living in seclusion on the top of Mount Kongtong, so he went to see him.

"Master," said the Yellow Emperor, "I have heard that you have found the perfect Tao. What is the essence of the perfect Tao? May I grasp the essence of Heaven and Earth and use them to assist the harvesting of the five crops in order to help the people? Moreover, how can I direct Yin and Yang and conform to the nature of all things?"

Guang Cheng Zi replied, "What you ask about is the true element of all things; what you want to achieve is the essence of all things. Since you began governing the world, clouds and air have not formed, and yet it rains; the trees and bushes drop their leaves before their time. This is because the weather is not right and the sun and moon are in disharmony. You are a man whose heart has become numbed by words; you are insubstantial and feeble. Consequently, you are not fit to be taught the Tao."

The Yellow Emperor returned, whereupon he ceased ruling the world. He constructed a room of silence and he sat on a white grass mat for three months undisturbed. He then visited Guang Cheng Zi again, and found him lying down facing south. The Yellow Emperor, with an air of deference, came forward on his knees, saying, "Last time I did not learn the Tao, would you mind teaching me the way of cultivation today?"

Guang Cheng Zi stood up and let the Yellow Emperor approach closer. "You are close to it," he said. "Let me teach you. The essence of the perfect Tao is hidden in darkness, lost in silence. It can not be seen or heard. Embrace the spirit in quietness, the body with its own rightness. Be still, be pure, do not make your body struggle, do not disturb your essence. The eye does not see, the ear does not hear, the heart knows nothing. Then your spirit and body will be one. Your body will live a long time and your heart will be strong. You do not recognize, nor realize, and are not influenced by the outer world, yet your virtues are complete. Much use of the heart and brain cannot help but use up the body. I will go with you to the great universe to let you feel the perfect Yang; I will go with you to the nether world to let you experience the perfect Yin. Then you may have the complete experience that Nature, and the sun, moon and stars —everything under Heaven—have those who rule them, and Yin and Yang have their places of concealment. Guard and take care of your body, and you need not worry about anything. I sustain unity and dwell in harmony, thus have I remained alive for 1,200 years, and my body has not aged."

The Yellow Emperor bowed his head to the ground twice and asked, "Have you not become one with Heaven?"

Guang Cheng Zi said, "The changes in everything are inexhaustible, but people still think that there is an end. The one who follows my Tao will be supreme in Heaven; if down below, he will be a king. The one who fails to follow my Tao will be able to see the brightness above but will become mere soil in the end. Every creature born comes from the soil and returns to the soil. He who follows my Tao can travel in the fields of the boundless with no limit and can return to the limitless place, can combine with the sun and the moon and live as long as Heaven and Earth. His heart is like a clean mirror reflecting the signs of the nether world. He who keeps clear of my Tao will be confused and ignorant. All the people may die, but I alone will survive!"

The Yellow Emperor said nothing, as if understanding something.

"Leaving the World Open," *The Outer Chapters of Zhuang Zi*

Note: *He who thinks he is more important than a governor of the world can not govern the world. So when the Yellow Emperor asked Guang Cheng Zi how to govern the world, he refused to answer. When he asked about longevity, Guang Cheng Zi said: "Be still, be pure, do not make your body struggle." That is to say, let the country develop as it will, neither restraining nor propelling it—in other words, government by non-action.*

9. Confucius Seeks to Store His Works in the Royal Library

The educator and founder of Confucianism, Confucius (551-479 B.C.), wanted to store his works in the archives of the Royal House of Western Zhou. His disciple Zi Lu suggested, "I have heard that the official in charge of the Royal Archives, Lao Dan (Lao Zi), has retired and lives at home. Sir, if you want to place your books there, why not ask his assistance?"

"Good idea," said Confucius.

So Confucius took his works with him and went to see Lao Zi. But Lao Zi gave no response to his discourse. So Confucius leafed through his works to find more explanations. Lao Zi interrupted him, saying, "Your arguments are tedious; get to the point!"

Confucius said, "Well, in essence, what I stress in my writings are benevolence and righteousness."

"May I ask, " said Lao Zi, "are benevolence and righteousness of the very essence of humanity?"

"Certainly," said Confucius. "If the nobleman is without benevolence, he makes no achievement; if without righteousness, he can not remain in society. Benevolence and righteousness are both a nobleman's personality and a human being's nature. How else could it be?"

"What exactly are benevolence and righteousness?"

"To be at one, centered in one's heart, loving all without selfishness. That is what benevolence and righteousness are," replied Confucius.

Lao Zi, frowningly, said, "Preposterous! Don't you think 'loving all without selfishness' is both vague and an exaggeration? By demanding that others be unselfish, you are seeking to allow yourself to be selfish. You ask that all people retain their education and have benevolent and righteous natures at the same time. That is tantamount to denying the following: Heaven and Earth exist; the sun and moon already give brightness; the stars and planets have their fixed order; the birds and beasts have formed their herds and flocks; and the trees have formed their forests. So Sir, I would advise you to follow Nature's laws in all your actions and words. It is perverse to trumpet this so-called benevolence and righteousness stuff, which goes against man's very nature. You want to deposit your works in the royal archives, hoping that thus your ideas on benevolence and righteousness will be more widely disseminated. But that would be like beating a drum in pursuit of a fugitive: The louder you beat it, the further away he runs! The more you go on about benevolence and righteousness, the more unattainable these virtues become. In this way, are you not poisoning men's minds and confusing their intrinsic natures?

"The Tao of Heaven," *The Outer Chapters of Zhuang Zi*

Note: *The author stresses that pursuit of the benevolence and righteousness advocated by Confucius serves only to lead people astray from the path of their true natures.*

10. The Lord of the Yellow River Learns Humility

The waters began to flow with the spring thaw, and by autumn had become raging floods. By then Yang (the positive, male principle) began to wane, while Yin (the negative, female principle) began to wax. It rained constantly, and the morning and evening tides grew ever fiercer. The mountain torrents pouring into the Yellow River swelled it so much that, gazing from one bank, one could not tell whether an animal on the farther bank was a cow or a horse.

One day the Lord of the Yellow River took a tour of his realm. Everything he saw pleased him, and he thought that the most beautiful thing in the whole world—the mighty Yellow River—belonged to him. Flowing with the river, he traveled its whole length. When he came at last to the sea, he looked east and could see no end to the waters. Crestfallen, he said to Ruo, the God of the North Sea, who had come to meet him:

"The saying, 'He who has heard of the Tao thinks he is superior to everyone else,' is certainly apposite in my case. I always used to consider that Confucius was a great scholar for he revised and compiled the Six Books; Bo Yi gave up his throne to practice benevolence and righteousness. I never set store by those wiseacres who belittled Confucius and Bo Yi, but now that I have seen your endless vastness, I realize that their criticism is reasonable. Fortunately, you have opened my eyes and broadened my understanding. Otherwise, I, in my self-conceit, would have become a permanent laughing-stock."

The God Ruo replied, "A frog which lives in a well cannot discuss the dimensions of Heaven and Earth, because its universe is bounded by the size of the well; a summer insect cannot discuss the ice and frost of winter, because it knows only its own season; a narrow-minded man cannot discuss the Tao, because he is constrained by the Confucian ethical code and the doctrine of benevolence. Now you have left the confines of your own domain and seen the Great Sea. You have shed your self-conceit, and so it is now possible to discuss great principles with you.

"Under Heaven there are no greater waters than those of the sea. All rivers flow into it day and night, ceaselessly. But it never overflows, for the water disappears at Wei Lu. Spring and autumn bring no changes. It pays no attention to floods or droughts. It is impossible to estimate how much water comes to me, but I am never smug and complacent about this. Compared to Heaven and Earth, I am only a tiny mite. I am just one of the myriad things formed by the dual action of Yin and Yang. I am like a pebble on a vast expanse of land or a shrub in a mighty forest. What do I have to be puffed up about? Moreover, I am just one of the four seas, which themselves, compared with Heaven and Earth, are of no more account than an anthill in a marsh.

"Human beings inhabit part of the land within the four seas. This land is no bigger than a grain of rice in a huge granary in comparison to Heaven and Earth. On this tiny land there are tens of thousands of living things, and humanity is just one of them. All living things are here; grain grows in the soil; boats float on the water; and carriages trundle along the roads. Humanity is just one portion of all life, in comparison to which is it not just like the tip of a single hair on a horse? What the Five Emperors (the Yellow Emperor, Zhuan Xu, Di Shou, Tang Yao and Yu Shun) modestly declined, the Three Kings (King Tang of Shang, King Wen of Zhou and King Wu of Zhou) fought over, officials struggle for, and benevolent people worry about is nothing more than this. Bo Yi is considered famous because he gave up the throne. Confucius is known as scholarly because he taught the Six Books. In their overweening self-glorification were they not just like you, who used to be so proud of yourself?"

"Autumn Flood," *The Outer Chapters of Zhuang Zi*

Note: *Big and small, deep and shallow must be identified by comparison. Some are proud of their bigness, for they don't know how big the world is. Through the comparisons between the sea and the Yellow River, Heaven and a single hair, the author points out that from the viewpoint of the Tao everything is the same, no matter whether it is big or small, high or low, right or wrong.*

11. Singing and Drumming on a Tub

When Zhuang Zi's wife died, Hui Zi came to console him. He found Zhuang Zi sitting at his ease and singing, all the time drumming on an old tub. Nonplused, Hui Zi said, "You lived as man and wife, she reared your children. But now that she has died, you do not weep for her, but sit there singing and banging away on a tub in this preposterous fashion!"

Zhuang Zi said, "You don't understand. When she died, at first I certainly did mourn. However, I then thought back to her birth and to the very roots of her being, before she was born. Indeed, not to just before she was born but to before the time when her body was created. Not to just before her body was created but to before the very origin of her life's breath. Out of all this, through the wonderful mystery of change, she was given her life's breath. From her life's breath, she gained a body and was born. Now she has gone from life to death—just like the four seasons follow each other. She is now at peace, lying in her chamber. Why should I weep like common people who do not comprehend the changes of nature? Why should I not bang on the tub and sing in appreciation of her luck?"

Hui Zi left without saying a word.

"Perfect Happiness," *The Outer Chapters of Zhuang Zi*

Note: *From his own experience, Zhuang Zi explains his attitude to life and death. In his view, life comes from breath and must become breath again when it expires. It is futile to grieve over a person's death, for life and death are perfectly natural changes of state.*

12. The Tree and the Goose

Zhuang Zi and his disciples were walking in the mountains, when they saw some woodcutters standing beside a huge flourishing tree.

Zhuang Zi asked them why they did not chop it down. One of the woodcutters replied, "Although this tree is a big one, its wood is not good material. So it would be a waste of time to chop it down."

"Just so," said Zhuang Zi. "Because this tree is useless, it is allowed to live out all the years Heaven has allotted to it."

Emerging from the mountains, Zhuang Zi and his disciples went to spend a night at a friend's house. His friend was delighted to see them and told his servant to kill a goose for their supper.

The servant said, "There are two geese; one can cackle, the other one can't. Which one should I kill?"

His master replied, "Kill the one that cannot cackle."

The next day, as they continued on their way, his disciples asked Zhuang Zi: "The tree we saw in the mountains can live all the years Heaven gave it just because it is of no use. But yesterday, at your friend's house, a goose died precisely because it was of no use. Why then were opposite fates granted to two equally useless things? Moreover, how are we to distinguish the useful from the useless?"

Zhuang Zi laughed and said, "A useful thing has usefulness, a useless thing has not. I'd find a position between usefulness and uselessness. This position between usefulness and uselessness might seem a good position and be close to the Tao, but it is not the Tao, so trouble will still come to you. It would certainly not be so, if you were to mount upon the Virtue of the Tao. That is to say, you should never be directed, praised and condemned, like a dragon flowing in the air or a snake staying in seclusion, following the change of nature without any thought of self. Let things be, but don't allow things to treat you as just an object, then you cannot be led into difficulties! The useful with much more use will be destroyed. The worthy with benevolence must want to be used, so they must fall a prey to a plot; people without ability want to be used, they must be insulted for their overrating themselves. You asked me how to deal with people and things, in my opinion, you need not chase for the useful. Remember, follow the change of nature, that's the Tao and its Virtue!"

"The Huge Tree," *The Outer Chapters of Zhuang Zi*

Note: *Only when you let things be will you not be led into difficulties.*

13. The Mantis Stalks the Cicada

While strolling through the park named Diaoling, Zhuang Zi saw a strange bird come flying from the south. Its wing-span measured seven feet and its eyes were large, about an inch in diameter. It brushed against Zhuang Zi's forehead and then alighted in a copse of chestnut trees. Zhuang Zi said to himself: "What sort of bird is this, with wings so vast but going nowhere, eyes so large but unable to see properly?" Hitching up his robe, he hurried after it with his crossbow in order to take a pot shot at it. On the way he saw a cicada basking in the grass. Just at that time, a playing mantis was stretching forth its feelers and preparing to spring upon the cicada, so engrossed in the hunt that it forgot its own safety. The strange bird swept down and seized them both, likewise forgetting its own safety. Zhuang Zi sighed with compassion and said, "So it is that one thing brings disaster upon another, and then upon itself!" He cast aside his crossbow and turned to leave the park, whereupon the park keeper upbraided him under the misapprehension that he was there to steal chestnuts.

Zhuang Zi went home and refused to go out again

for three months. When Lin Cu, one of his disciples, asked him the reason for his low spirits, Zhuang Zi said, "Safety and danger exist side by side. But people are so obsessed with the safety of their persons that they forget the environment they find themselves in. Today, I was so concerned with my body that I forgot my surroundings. It was like looking into cloudy water, thinking it was really clear. My teacher, Lao Dan, told me: 'When associating with the locals, act like a local,' When I went out walking in Diaoling Park I forgot his teaching. So when a strange jackdaw touched my forehead and then settled in a copse of chestnut trees, I forgot all about the rules of the park. The commotion brought the park keeper's wrath upon me. That is why I am miserable."

"The Huge Tree," *The Outer Chapters of Zhuang Zi*

Note: *Those who do not plan for the future will find trouble on their doorsteps; those who forget themselves when pursuing their own interests are storing up trouble for themselves. Only when we take the whole situation into account can we avoid one-sidedness and keep our fundamental interests.*

14. No Need for Words

Wen Xue Zi, a man from the State of Chu (in south-central China) who had acquired the Tao, once went to the State of Qi (on the Shandong Peninsula). On the way, he stopped in the nearby State of Lu. A follower of Confucius asked to see him, but he refused. When his servant asked him why, he said, "The people from the Central Plains are clear about the principles of ritual, but dull in their understanding of people's hearts. I do not wish to see him."

He duly arrived in Qi, but on his way back home he passed once more through the domain of Lu, and the follower of Confucius called on him again. This time Wen Xue Zi decided to find out the persistent fellow's intentions.

He went out to see the visitor, but came back sighing. The next day, he saw the visitor again, and again came back sighing. His servant asked him, "Why is it, sir, that whenever you see that person, you come back sighing?"

He replied, "I told you before, 'The people from the Central Plains are clear about the principles of ritual, but dull in their understanding of people's hearts.' The visitor is well-mannered and behaves in a fit and proper way. But his appearance is like that of a dragon or a tiger. He rebukes me as if he were my father. I can not bear it, and that is why I sigh."

Two days later, Confucius went to see him but did not say a word. His disciple Zi Lu said, "Sir, you have often wished to visit Wen Xue Zi, yet when you saw him you did not say a word. Why?"

"As soon as I saw him, I could see the Tao," said Confucius. "There was no need for words."

"Tian Zifang," *The Outer Chapters of Zhuang Zi*

Note: *In this story, through the words of Wen Xue Zi, the author mocks the Confucianists for being masters of ritual, but having little understanding of people's hearts.*

15. Fancy But Useless Archery

Lie Zi, from the State of Zheng, was showing off his archery skill to Bo Hun Wu Ren, a hermit from the State of Chu. To demonstrate how steady he was, he balanced a cup brimful of water on his left elbow while he was shooting.

No sooner had one arrow left the bowstring than another was ready to be shot, followed by a third at the ready, and so on. And all this time Lie Zi stood as still as a statue, spilling not a drop of the water. Bo Hun Wu Ren said, "This is indeed fancy archery. But your skill is a hollow one. Let us see if you can shoot arrows so well from the edge of a precipice!"

Lie Zi accepted the challenge, and the two set off to scale a nearby peak. When they reached the edge of a steep cliff Bo Hun Wu Ren turned round and walked backward toward the drop until his feet were half over the edge. Thereupon he bowed to Lie Zi and asked him to join him. Lie Zi fell to the ground in terror, sweat pouring from him. Bo Hun Wu Ren said, "The perfect man can stare at the azure Heavens above or go down into the Earth below, or journey away to the eight ends of the cosmos without his spirit and original breath being affected in any way whatsoever. But look at you, trembling, paralyzed and with your eyes popping out of your head with fear!"

"Tian Zifang," *The Outer Chapters of Zhuang Zi*

Note: *This story highlights the fact that no matter how wonderful one's skill, it vanishes as soon as one thinks of life and death, or loss and gain.*

16. Knowledge Journeys to the North

Knowledge was interested in finding out about the Tao. Knowing little about it, he asked everyone he met.

One day he wandered north to the shores of the Dark Waters, climbed to the top of the Secret Heights and there came upon Words-of-Actionless-Action. Knowledge said to Words-of-Actionless-Action: "I am so glad to meet you, for I wish to enquire, first, what sort of thought and reflection does it take to know the Tao? Second, in what sort of place and in what sort of ways should we undertake to rest in the Tao? And, third, which path and what method do we need to obtain the Tao?"

Words-of-Actionless-Action did not answer these three questions. Not only did he not answer, he had no idea what to answer.

Having failed to obtain any answers, Knowledge traveled to the White Waters of the south, climbed to the top of desolate Mount Huque, and there caught sight of Wild-and-Surly. Knowledge put the same questions to Wild-and-Surly, who thought a while, and said, "I know, and I will tell you."

But no sooner had he said this than he forgot what he was going to tell Knowledge.

Words-of-Actionless-Action, who was in a dark and unclear situation, could not answer questions about the Tao; Wild-and-Surly, who was in an empty and clear situation, wanted to answer but forgot what he wanted to say. And so, Knowledge failed to obtain any answers.

He thereupon went to see the Yellow Emperor, and put the same questions to him.

The Yellow Emperor replied with six "no's": "With no thoughts and no reflections, you will come to know the Tao. In no place and no way, you will find rest in the Tao. Have no path and no methods, and you will obtain the Tao."

Knowledge said, "The Tao seems so simple to you. But it was not simple for the others I asked. So which of the three of you is actually right?"

The Yellow Emperor said, "Words-of-Actionless-Action was truly right, but he did not know it. Wild-and-Surly thought he was right, but he forgot what he was going to say. You and I are not close to it, for we talk about the Tao. Those who understand it do not speak about it. Those who speak about it do not understand it. And so the sage follows the teachings without words. The Tao cannot be made to occur, and virtue cannot be sought. However, benevolence can be undertaken, righteousness can be striven for and rituals can be adhered to. When the Tao was lost, virtue appeared; when virtue was lost, benevolence appeared; when benevolence was lost, righteousness appeared; and when righteousness was lost, ritual appeared. Rituals are just the frills on the hem of the Tao, and are signs of impending disorder. One who would follow the Tao should cast away empty show and dishonesty; only then can he eventually arrive at actionless action. Having achieved actionless action, there is nothing which can not be done.

"Otherwise, if we wish to return to our original state, we will find it very difficult. Who but the great man could change this? Life follows death, and death is the forerunner of life. Human life begins with the original breath; when it comes together, there is life, and when it disappears, there is death. If people knew this, they would not worry about personal gains and losses.

"Death and life are one. All things living must experience death, in a process of flourishing and decaying. All forms of life are one. Yet we regard some as beautiful, because they are spiritual and wonderful; others we count as ugly, because they are diseased and rotting. But the diseased and rotting can become the spiritual and wonderful, and the spiritual and wonderful can become the diseased and rotting. In the eyes of the Tao, there is no beautiful or ugly thing—everything under Heaven is one breath. The sages comprehended such unity."

Knowledge said to the Yellow Emperor: "I asked

Words-of-Actionless-Action, and he did not say anything to me. Indeed, he did not know what to say to me. I asked Wild-and-Surly, and he was just about to explain when he suddenly forgot what he wanted to say. Then I asked you, and you know the answer. So why do you say you are not close to the Tao?"

The Yellow Emperor replied, "Words-of-Actionless-Action was actually right. He who really knows the Tao can not speak it out. Wild-and-Surly was almost right, because he forgot everything. However, you and I just explain the Tao with our wisdom. The Tao comes from nature, which can not be talked about. That which can be talked about is not the real Tao, not even close to the edge of the Tao."

When Wild-and-Surly learned of the conversation between Knowledge and the Yellow Emperor, he was convinced by the Yellow Emperor's words.

"Knowledge Journeys to the North," *The Outer Chapters of Zhuang Zi*

Note: *This fable stresses the futility of asking about the Tao. Talk is not better than wanting to speak, wanting to speak is not better than saying nothing. He who says nothing knows the Tao, for the Tao is emptiness; it can't be asked about, spoken about or seen. Only he who is speechless and actionless can achieve the Tao.*

17. The Tao Can Be Found Even in Dung

Shun Zi, who lived in the same town as Zhuang Zi, one day asked Zhuang Zi: "Where is that ethereal thing called the Tao?"

Zhuang Zi replied, "It can be found in anything."

"Please explain further."

"It is in this ant."

"Is that its lowest point?"

"No, it is in this blade of grass."

"Can you give me a lower example?"

"It is in this common earthenware tile."

"This must be its lowest point!"

"Not at all; the Tao can be found even in dung," said Zhuang Zi.

This answer left Shun Zi dumbfounded.

Zhuang Zi explained, "Sir, your questions miss the point. Once upon a time a market inspector named Huo asked his superintendents how to test the value of a pig. They told him that the lower down the animal you pressed, the closer you were to find the truth. So you should not look for the Tao in anything specific. There is nothing that lacks it.

"You can not talk about the Tao separately from things. Complete, all-embracing, universal: three different words but with the same reality, all referring back to the one. Imagine that in endless and distant space all these words have no comparison, not to mention high and low, above and below, much and less. Everything has no end, no limit, and no body at all.

"Actionless action exists in simplicity and quietude, in disinterest and purity, in harmony and ease. My intentions are now aimless. I do not know where to go or whither to return; I go and I come, and don't know why. I have been, I have gone. I have no idea when my journey will be over. But only great men who can wander in unlimited vastness have such experiences. They master the changes of things and follow the changes by making no distinctions. If you can regard things as simply things, then you do not share the limited nature of things. The limitation arises out of the limited, and the boundless arises out of the restricted. We talk of fullness and emptiness, of withering and decaying. The Tao makes them full or empty, but is not defined by fullness or emptiness. It creates withering and decay, but it is defined by neither root nor branch. It gathers together and it disappears, but it is neither of these itself."

After this, Zhuang Zi left.

"Knowledge Journeys to the North," *The Outer Chapters of Zhuang Zi*

Note: *This story explains that there is nowhere where the Tao is not, and there is nothing that lacks it. Zhuang Zi makes the point that the Tao can be found in the lowest substance, for he wants people to understand that the Tao is not mysterious and it never follows people's will.*

18. Weeping Over a Prediction of Fortune

Zi Qi, minister of war of King Zhuang of the State of Chu (reigned 613-591 B.C.), had eight sons. One day he called them before him, and summoned Jiu Fang Yin, a hermit skilled in metoposcopy, and said to him: "Study the physiognomies of my sons, and tell me which one is to be the most fortunate?"

"Kun will be the most fortunate, " said Jiu Fang Yin.

"How so?" Zi Qi asked.

"Kun will dine with the ruler of a kingdom until the end of his days," came the reply.

Tears poured from Zi Qi's eyes, and he moaned: "Why does my son deserve such a fate?"

Jiu Fang Yin was surprised. "One who shares the table of a ruler of a kingdom brings blessings upon his whole family, and especially upon his parents!"

Zi Qi retorted, "How do you know that this will be good fortune for Kun? The food and drink only touches the mouth, so how can one claim to know where they come from? I have never been a shepherd, but a lamb appeared in the southwest corner of my house; I have never been a hunter, but a flock of quails have been hung in the southeast corner of my house. Strange indeed! I and my sons live happily under Heaven and we look for nourishment from Earth. I don't want them to get caught up in the affairs of the world, especially in plots and strange practices. We follow the Tao of Heaven and Earth and let nothing come between us. We are one in undisturbed unity, and we are not interested in doing what others think would be useful. Now the world must be preparing to take its vengeance on us. In my experience, when something untoward happens, it is the result of something untoward having been done. This is not our fault, so it must come from Heaven! That is what makes me weep."

Not long after this, Zi Qi sent Kun on an errand to the State of Yan. On the way, he was captured by bandits. They decided to cut off his feet and sell him as a slave. They did this, and sold him in the State of Qi, where the ruler needed a manservant. So, just as had been predicted Kun had food to sustain him until the end of his days.

"Xu Wu Gui," *The Miscellaneous Chapters of Zhuang Zi*

Note: *Zi Qi and his son's experience indicates that even those who follow the Tao of Heaven may still have trouble.*

19. Craftsman Shi Whirls His Axe

Zhuang Zi was following a funeral, when he passed by the grave of Hui Zi, who had had a reputation as a fine debater. He turned to his disciples, and said, "A man of Ying, the capital of the State of Chu, once had on the end of his nose a piece of mud as small as a spot on a fly's wing. He asked Craftsman Shi to remove it. Shi whirled his axe and swept it down, creating such a wind as it rushed past that it removed all traces of the mud from the nose of the man of Ying, who stood firm, not at all worried. Duke Yuan of Song heard of this, and summoned Craftsman Shi. "'Would you be so kind as to demonstrate your skill for me?' he said.

"Craftsman Shi replied, 'Indeed I have magical skill. But to utilize it, I must work with my best partner. Now he has died, and so has my skill.'"

Heaving a sigh, Zhuang Zi continued, "Since Hui Zi has died, I have not had any suitable material to work upon. I have no one I can talk with any longer."

"Xu Wu Gui," *The Miscellaneous Chapters of*

Zhuang Zi

Note: *This anecdote indicates that if people who get along well and have well-matched companions cooperate with and learn from each other they can give their skills full play; otherwise their skills will wither.*

20. The Turtle Oracle

Duke Yuan of Song (reigned 531-516 B.C.) once dreamed that a man with disheveled hair peered in at him through his bedroom window and said, "I used to be the administrator of the deep waters of Yuanlutan, and on my way from the Yangtze River as an ambassador to the Lord of the Yellow River a fisherman called Yu Cu caught me. I beg Your Majesty to save my life."

Duke Yuan woke up, and immediately sent for a diviner to find out what this portended. "It was a sacred turtle," said the diviner. The duke then asked whether there was a fisherman named Yu Cu, and being told that there was, he commanded that the man be brought before him.

When Yu Cu arrived, the duke asked him: "What have you caught recently?"

The man replied, "A huge white turtle, Your Majesty."

Thereupon, Duke Yuan ordered Yu Cu to hand over the turtle, which he did.

For a while the duke was at a loss what to do with the creature. Then the diviner came up with an idea:

"Why not kill it and use its shell for divinations?" he suggested.

Duke Yuan had the turtle killed and its shell used for divinations. Seventy-two times in a row the shell delivered oracles which proved to be accurate.

When Confucius heard about the miraculous turtle shell, he said to his disciples:

"The sacred turtle could ask for help from Lord Yuan, but could not escape the nets of Yu Cu. It had sufficient wisdom to give seventy-two correct divinations, but it could not predict that the ruler would kill it instead of saving it. It seems that all things can do their best, but they can not guarantee the actions of others. Wisdom has its limits, and even spirituality finds something beyond its reach. Even perfect wisdom can be defeated by scheming people. Fish seem not to fear nets; they only seem to fear pelicans. Nets, without feeling, always catch some, but pelicans, driven by desire, often get nothing. People flock to pettifogging soothsayers. Rid yourself of petty knowledge, and allow wisdom to enlighten you. Rid yourself of goodness, and goodness will naturally arise. When a child is born, it needs no great teacher; nevertheless it learns to talk, as it lives with those who talk."

"Outer Things," *The Miscellaneous Chapters of Zhuang Zi*

Note: *As even a sacred turtle, which can foretell the future, may misjudge a key matter, people who are extremely intelligent may be ensnared by others. The best way to proceed is to forget wisdom and do nothing.*

21. Hiding One's Sickness for Fear of Treatment

The physician Bian Que went to see Marquis Huan of the State of Cai (reigned 514-495 B.C.). After a while, he said to the ruler: "Your Majesty, you are afflicted with a disease, but, as yet, it is only skin-deep. I urge you to take a course of treatment immediately. If you do not, the disease will only get worse."

Marquis Huan smiled and said, "I am suffering from no illness."

After Bian Que left, Marquis Huan said to his ministers: "These quacks are always treating people who are not sick. They are trying to show off, I suppose."

Ten days later, Bian Que visited the marquis again, and urged him, "Your Majesty, your disease has already progressed to your muscles and blood vessels. If no treatment is given, your condition will only get worse."

Marquis Huan still did not believe he was sick, and angrily dismissed the physician.

Ten days later, when Bian Que saw the marquis again, his diagnosis was somber: "The disease has invaded your internal organs. If no treatment is ad-

ministered, the consequences could be serious indeed!"

This time the marquis flew into a rage.

Another ten days later, when Bian Que saw Marquis Huan in the distance, he ran and disappeared like a whirlwind. Puzzled, Marquis Huan sent someone to ask Bian Que the reason for his odd behavior.

Bian Que said to him: "At first, His Majesty's disease was only at the level of the skin, and an ointment would have been sufficient to cure it. Later, when the disease had progressed to the muscles and internal organs, acupuncture or a medicinal concoction could have cured it. But now that His Majesty's disease has penetrated his bones, I am afraid that nothing more can be done."

Five days later, Marquis Huan's whole body was suddenly racked with pain, and Bian Que was hastily sent for. However, by this time the physician had already moved to the State of Qin.

A good doctor always begins his treatment of a disease from the skin in order to nip it in the bud. Anything, fortune or misfortune, develops from small to big. Wise people take countermeasures at the very beginning.

"Yu Lao, " *Han Fei Tzu*

Note: *A serious disease develops from a minor one. It is important to identify a disease at the very outset. Then we* *should seek treatment as soon as possible, or the disease will get out of control. Everything has its own process of emergence and development. If we can find its origin and grasp its development trend, we can influence it from the very beginning, and lead it in the direction we desire.*

22. The Lost Axe

A person who believes a one-sided story or hearsay ends up bigoted and limited in imagination. Bigotry and limitation will always lead people astray. Such a person knows only the east, but not the west; he watches only the south, but not the north. A story which illustrates this goes as follows:

Once upon a time there was a craftsman who lost his axe. He thought hard, and finally suspected his neighbor of stealing it. When he saw his neighbor walking, he thought that he walked like an axe thief. When he met his neighbor, the other's countenance was just like that of an axe thief, and when he saw him in conversation with others, he even talked like an axe thief!

Not long afterward, the craftsman found his axe where he had mislaid it. Strangely enough, from that time on, his neighbor ceased to walk, look and talk like an axe thief!

"Qu You," *Master Lu's Spring and Autumn Annals*

Note: *The author points out that when a man watches only the east he cannot see the west; when he watches only the south he cannot see the north, for he pays attention only to one side, to the neglect of the other sides. To judge a thing, it is not enough to guess and ignore the facts. But some people have the habit of subjectively creating images and being prejudiced against others. This is completely wrong.*

23. Cheng Zi Loses His Jacket

A man called Cheng Zi of the State of Song lost a black jacket. Looking for it along the road, he saw a woman wearing a black jacket coming toward him. He claimed that the jacket was his, and demanded that she hand it over.

The woman said, "But this can't be your jacket, for I made it myself."

Thereupon, Cheng Zi said, "My jacket was made of silk; yours is made of cotton. Is it not worth exchanging your cotton jacket for my silk one?"

"Lewd Expressions," *Master Lu's Spring and Autumn Annals*

Note: *The point of this story is that Cheng Zi was so absorbed in his own loss that he abandoned logic completely. Some people who do harm put all the blame on others and are blind to their own faults.*

24. Chimes Heard at Night

The Spring and Autumn Period (770-476 B.C.) musician Zhong Ziqi heard a set of stone chimes being played one night. The tune was so mournful that he was overwhelmed by its haunting tone. He sent for the person playing the chimes, and said to him: "Your melody was so sad that I fear you must harbor some crushing sorrow."

The man said, "Three years ago, my father accidentally killed a person, and paid with his life. At the same time, my mother was sold into slavery, and I was forced to earn my living as a wondering musician playing the stone chimes. I sorely miss my mother. Not long ago, I met her at a market and wanted to redeem her. But I myself am in servitude; how can I redeem my mother? Whenever I think of it, I despair."

Hearing this, Zhong Ziqi sighed: "How sad it is! A man's heart is different from his arm, and his arm is different from the stick for playing the stone chimes. But when a person is sad, the sorrow in his heart can be expressed by the stones themselves!"

Then Zhong Ziqi ordered his servant to redeem the man.

"Mastery," *Master Lu's Spring and Autumn Annals*

Note: *Like attracts like. The man who played the stone chimes was lucky to meet a talented musician like Zhong Ziqi, who knew what his music wanted to say.*

25. Shi Kuang Checks the Bells

The difference between a mediocre person and a person of genius is that the latter can think back one thousand years and think ahead one thousand years.

During the Spring and Autumn Period, Duke Ping of Jin (reigned 557-532 B.C.) had a large musical instrument, which consisted of several groups of bells, made. When it was finished, the duke ordered his head court musician to check the tones of the bells.

Several days later, the duke invited Shi Kuang, another musician, to try out the instrument. Tapping one or two bells, Shi Kuang said to the duke: "They are not in harmony. You will have to cast them anew."

The duke was surprised and protested, "But my head court musician has already tested the bells, and pronounced them perfect!"

Shi Kuang said, "He checked their tones according to the ancient scales. Later generations will develop new scales, and then both you and I will be mocked for our lack of musical knowledge."

Several years later, another musician, Shi Juan, really did criticize the bells' tones.

Shi Kuang was skilled enough at distinguishing tones that he knew not only the current and past ones, but also future ones. That was the difference between him and ordinary musicians.

"Far-sightedness," *Master Lu's Spring and Autumn Annals*

Note: *In the author's opinion, past, current and future are all connected in a linear way. Shi Kuang had both ancient and modern learning, and could project his knowledge into the future.*

26. Jiu Fang Yin Judges Horses

Duke Mu of the State of Qin (reigned 659-621 B.C.) asked Bo Le, who was skillful at judging horses: "Sir, you are old now; can your son take your job over from you?"

Bo Le replied, "To judge a horse, you must observe its looks, muscles and bones. It is not easy to find fine horses. When you find one, you may look at its appearance and overlook its spirit, or vice versa. Without one of these two points, it will not be a fine horse. My son is not good at judging horses, Sire. But if you want to find a person who really can judge fine horses, I recommend Jiu Fang Yin, who used to cut wood with me. His skill surpasses mine."

The duke summoned Jiu Fang Yin, and told him to find the most superb horses in the world.

Jiu Fang Yin went off on his search. Three months later, he was back in the capital, and reported to the ruler: "Sire, I have found a fine horse for you."

The duke asked, "What kind of a horse is it?"

Jiu Fang Yin said, "A roam stallion."

The duke sent a servant to fetch the horse, and found that it was a black mare. So he sent for Bo Le,

and complained, "This is ridiculous! Jiu Fang Yin is color blind, and, moreover, he cannot tell a mare from a stallion. A fine judge of horses you recommended to me!"

Bo Le said, "Your Majesty is mistaken. Jiu Fang Yin is far superior to me in judging horses. He can see nature's mystery that others cannot see. Nature's mystery lies in minute, hidden places, not on the surface; the interior should be studied, while appearance can be ignored; key points must be focused on, while unnecessary parts may be put aside. Jiu Fang Yin has judged the key point and ignored the unnecessary parts. So the horse he found must be a rare one."

The duke ordered a skilled horseman to ride the horse. It turned out that it was a rare animal after all.

"Taoist Teachings," *Huai Nan Zi*

Note: *Jiu Fang Yin could see what others could not. He could observe the essence and the interior, and grasp nature's mystery, whereas others could not. This story emphasizes that essence and main content are more important than surface qualities.*

27. Excess Leads to Loss

Confucius and his disciple Zi Gong were worshipping at the ancestral temple of Duke Huan (reigned 711-694 B.C.) of the State of Lu. Watching Zi Gong pour water into a sacrificial vessel, Confucius noticed that as soon as the vessel was full, it tilted. In a flash of inspiration, Confucius cried, "That is *Chi Ying*."

Zi Gong asked, "Sir, can you tell me what '*Chi Ying*' is?"

"'*Chi Ying*' is the principle of "excess leads to loss."

"How does excess lead to loss?" Zi Gong asked.

Confucius said, "Everything starts with birth, then grows, and dies in the end. It is the same with the human race. Extreme joy is followed by sorrow. For example, the sun sinks into the west after noon, and the moon wanes after being full in the middle of the month. So, wise people always show themselves as dull, and scholarly people always reveal themselves as being in possession of limited knowledge and scanty information. People who are brave and have wonderful military skill always show themselves as timid, while rich and noble people pretend to be poor. Likewise, people who are skillful at running the country are always modest and polite. The former Duke Huan of Lu followed these principles, and so kept the country at peace. He who goes against these principles will end up in trouble."

"Taoist Teachings," *Huai Nan Zi*

Note: *Even ancient Chinese people knew that conceit led to loss, while modesty brought benefits. A person basking in self-conceit will incur losses. If people who run the country are overweening, they will bring trouble to the country.*

28. Better to Light a Candle

Duke Ping of the State of Jin said to his blind musician Shi Kuang: "I am over seventy. It is too late for me to learn."

Shi Kuang said, "Since you know it is late, why don't you light a candle?"

The duke was displeased, and rebuked the man, saying, "What kind of impertinence is that?"

Shi Kuang said, "How would a poor blind subject dare to be impertinent to his master? I have heard that when you learn at a young age, it is like the sun in the morning; in middle age, like the sun at noon; in old age, like the light of a candle. But you should not despise the light of a candle. Is it not much better than walking in darkness?"

Thereupon, the duke smiled and said, "Exactly!"

"Jian Ben," *Shuo Yuan*

Note: *The musician Shi Kuang pointed out that, just as lighting a candle was much better than walking in darkness, it is better to spend one's few remaining years improving one's mind than in ignorance.*

29. Images Impart Wisdom

Lord Mengchang, a noble of the State of Qi, was determined to offer his services to the State of Qin. His aides all tried to prevent this, but to no avail. "I have heard all your arguments before," he said, "and I am not convinced. If any one of you has anything new to tell men, let him speak up. Otherwise, remain silent."

One of his household stepped forward, and, upon bing bidden to speak, said, "On my way here today, I passed the Zishui River. There I saw two images hovering above the water. One was made of clay, and the other of wood. I heard the latter say to the former: 'You are made of clay, and so any shower of rain will turn you into a mere dollop of mud." The clay image replied, 'That is true, if I meet rain I will return to nature. But how about you? You are made from the wood of a peach tree in the Eastern Garden. A shower of rain would have you floating off down the river to Heaven-knows-where.' Now, my Lord, you want to offer your services to the State of Qin, which is casting a greedy eye on the Central Plains. If you go, you will, like the images, be completely at the mercy of fate."

Lord Mengchang pondered awhile in his hall, and then left without a word. From then on, he never again talked about going to the State of Qin.

"Admonitions," *Garden of Anecdotes*

Note: *Lord Mengchang was self-willed and refused to listen to reason. But the vivid fable used by his retainer convinced him that going to Qin would be a rash step. So a pithy fable may be more forceful than a reasoned argument.*

30. The Talker and the Doer

During the Spring and Autumn Period a man called Wei Gong lived in Xiacai (today's Fengtai County, Anhui Province). One day, his neighbor heard him weeping and lamenting, and when he asked Wei Gong the reason for his distress, the latter said, "Our country is doomed. How can I not be heartbroken?"

The neighbor asked, "How do you know that?"

Wei Gong replied, "I have heard that when a person is dying, even the best doctor cannot help him; and when a country is dying, even the best strategy cannot save it. I have tried to advise our ruler many times, but he refused to listen. So I think our end is near."

Hearing this, the neighbor moved his whole family to the State of Chu.

Several years later, the ruler of Chu conquered Xia Cai. The commander of the Chu forces was none other than Wei Gong's erstwhile neighbor, and he inquired if Wei Gong was among the captives.

When Wei Gong was brought before him, he asked, "What brought you, such a wise man, to this misfortune?"

Wei Gong replied, "I brought it upon myself! For

words are the servants of action, and actions are the masters of words. You are able to take action, while I can only speak. No wonder I am in such a condition!"

The former neighbor interceded with the king on Wei Gong's behalf, and Wei Gong was freed.

"Tactics and Strategies," *Shuo Yuan*

Note: *This anecdote points out the fact that those who are good at planning may not be good at taking action: Some people are talkers, while others are doers. Wei Gong could foresee the downfall of Xia Cai, but he could not avoid the calamity himself. This story shows that foresight and planning are important, but they are useless if one cannot act upon them.*

31. Rewarding Those with Singed Hair

During the early years of the Western Han Dynasty (206 B.C.-A.D. 24) the commander-in-chief, Huo Guang, performed illustrious deeds. His descendants, however, led lives of luxury and debauchery. A later emperor (Xuandi, 73-49 B.C.) was warned by an upright minister named Xu Fu of the danger posed by the Huo family, but the ruler ignored Xu Fu's admonition.

Sure enough, it was not long before the Huo clan tried to stage a coup against the emperor. The coup was foiled, and the emperor honored and rewarded those who had helped to stamp out the rebellion. Xu Fu and his warning were forgotten, until friends of Xu Fu petitioned the emperor, using the following allegory:

"On a visit to a friend, a certain man noticed that firewood was piled near the chimney. He advised his friend to bend the chimney away from the firewood, and to stack the firewood further away, lest it catch fire from the red-hot chimney and burn the house down. But his friend neglected to do so. A few days later, the house actually did catch fire, and the man's neighbors all came rushing to put it out. When the fire had been doused, the man gave a feast for his heroic neighbors. Those with singed hair or fire-related injuries were seated in the place of honor. However, the man who had urged that the chimney be bent and the firewood moved away was not invited. If the householder had listened to his friend's advice, this fire would not have happened and the feast would not have been necessary. Surely, the man who gave the warning offered the greatest help. Why should only those who offered less help have been honored? If Your Majesty had heeded Xu Fu's warning, the revolt would have been avoided, and awards would not have been necessary."

Thereupon, Emperor Xuandi rewarded Xu Fu appropriately.

"Tactics and Strategies," *Shuo Yuan*

Note: *This story stresses the importance of taking preventive measures to avert trouble before it happens. Those who warn of impending danger perform a greater service than those who offer assistance after the calamity takes place.*

32. Happily Gleaning Leftovers

Lin Lei was nearly one hundred years old. One fine spring day, he went out into the fields to glean leftover ears of wheat. There he was espied by Confucius, who was on his way to the State of Wei. Confucius said to his followers: "That old man is worth talking to. Who would like to?"

Zi Gong approached Lin Lei, and said, "Sir, judging by your merry singing, you seem to be quite content picking up scraps that others have left behind."

Lin Lei kept on singing and walking, searching the ground all the time for ears of wheat. Zi Gong followed him, and asked why he was so contented.

"What do I have to regret?" retorted Lin Lei.

Zi Gong said, "Sir, you did not study in your young days, and had no occupation when you became an adult. Now you are old, with no wife or children; what makes you so happy that you sing with joy as you comb the ground for scraps of wheat?"

Lin Lei smiled and said, "Everyone has what makes me happy, but they worry about it. For although I did not study hard in my youth and had no occupation as an adult, I have lived a long life. And since I have no wife or children to grieve, I can die happily."

Zi Gong said, "Everyone wants to live a long life and is afraid of death. Why are you so happy, with death looming before you?"

Lin Lei said, "Death and life—one is to come, the other is to go. If I die here, it may be to live there. I know that death and life are the same, so how can I be seduced by common things and strive vainly for survival? Who knows but that death may be better than life?"

Zi Gong did not understand what he meant, so he told Confucius what he had heard.

Confucius said, "I know that this old man is worth talking to. But what he knows is not perfect."

"Tian Rui," *Lie Zi*

Note: *Lin Lei considered life and death as the same thing. This story teaches that people who strive vainly for life are distracted by common things. Lin Lei held himself aloof from the world and was happy. His attitude chimes in with Taoism's ideas of "nature" and "doing nothing."*

33. The Man of Qi Who Feared That the Sky Might Fall

There was a man in the State of Qi (today's Qixian County, Henan Province) who worried that the sky would fall upon him and the earth would cave in beneath him. He became so anxious that he could neither eat nor sleep. A friend tried to explain away his fears:

"The sky is just a huge mass of air. It permeates everywhere, and you come into contact with it every day. From morning till night you live in it. So how can you be worried that it might fall?"

The man asked, "If the sky is a mass of air, how about the sun, moon and stars?"

His friend said, "They are shining masses of air. Even if they fall out of the sky, no harm will come to you."

The man then asked, "What if the earth caves in?"

The other said, "The earth is nothing but dirt and rocks piled up. It extends in every direction. You walk, run and jump on the earth every day. Don't you think it's rather futile to worry about it caving in?"

The man of Qi was pleased to hear this, and his

friend was equally pleased to have allayed his fears.

Chang Lu Zi heard about this and called it ridiculous. He said, "Rainbows, clouds and fog, wind and rain, and the four seasons are all masses of air; the mountains, rivers and seas, metal and stone, fire and wood are all dirt and rocks piled up. If we know that these things are all masses of air and dirt and rocks, how can we say they will last forever? Compared with the limitless universe, Heaven and Earth are very tiny. But, compared to limited things, they are so huge. It is not necessary to worry about their being destroyed too soon, like the man of Qi did, but it is not right to say they can never be destroyed. Both Heaven and Earth are doomed to end some day, so it is quite reasonable for people to fear this."

When Lie Zi heard this, he smiled and said, "It is absurd on both of their parts. Nobody knows whether Heaven and Earth will be destroyed or not. The same is true of life and death: The living cannot know what will happen after death; the dead cannot know what happens to the living. People in the future cannot know the past; the past cannot know the future. How absurd to worry about whether the sky will fall or the earth open up!"

"Tian Rui," *Lie Zi*

Note: *Here we are urged to eschew needless worrying. Such* *fretting may cause people to bring trouble upon themselves and become dispirited and disoriented. Meanwhile, through the advisor's words, we are reminded that subjective one-sidedness can be avoided if we use our heads and analyze matters. But, the author himself sneers at both the man of Qi and his advisor. In his opinion, the fate of Heaven and Earth can not be known at all.*

34. The Dream Deer

A man of the State of Zheng (in the vicinity of today's Xinzheng City, Henan) came upon a deer while out cutting firewood. He then killed the deer and hid it. However, he immediately forgot the location. Thinking that he must have been dreaming, he told everyone he met on his way home about this queer experience.

One of the people he told the story to was curious, and went to look for the deer. Sure enough, it was hidden where the woodcutter had said he had been working.

He took the deer home to his wife, and told her what had happened. She said scornfully: "I don't believe that there was a woodcutter. Perhaps you dreamed about him."

The man replied, "I've got this deer, so I don't care whether he or I had the dream."

That night, the woodcutter dreamed of the place he had hidden the deer, and of the person who had found it and taken it away. The next day, he tracked him down and hauled him off to the county magistrate.

The county magistrate said, "Woodcutter, when you

got a real deer, you thought it had been a dream. Later, when you dreamed of the deer, you thought it was a fact. His wife said that he had taken the deer in a dream. So, nobody really got the deer. My judgment is that you should divide it between you."

The ruler of Zheng heard about this, and said, "Perhaps the county magistrate dreamed about dividing the deer!"

He asked his prime minister, who said, "I cannot judge whether it was a dream or not. Only the Yellow Emperor and Confucius could do that. But they are both dead. Who else could distinguish reality from dreams? The best step is let the county magistrate's judgment stand."

"King Mu of Zhou," *Lie Zi*

Note: *In this passage the author wants to say that there is no difference at all between dreams and reality, truth and falsehood.*

35. The Teacher of Immortality

Once upon a time, there was a man who claimed to be able to teach the secret of immortality. The ruler of the State of Yan (in present day northern Hebei and western Liaoning provinces) sent someone to learn from him. But before he had learned the secret, the teacher died. The ruler was so angry that he ordered the student put to death. But one of his trusted advisors intervened, saying, "What people most worry about is death; what people most care about is life. The man who said he knew how to live forever, lost his own life. So how could he have taught Your Majesty to live forever?"

Hearing this, the ruler countermanded his order.

At the same time, a man named Qi Zi, who had also wanted to learn the secret of immortality, sighed upon hearing of the teacher's death: "How unfortunate! I should have sought him out earlier." On hearing this, Fu Zi mocked him, saying, "How could you have learned to live forever from a man who could not even preserve his own life?"

Hu Zi heard of this, and said, "What Fu Zi said is also not right. Some know the Tao, but cannot practice it; some could practice the Tao if they only knew how. There was a man in the State of Wei who was an expert at calculation. He taught this skill to his son before he died. But his son only knew the way; he could not put it to use. Others came to him to learn it, and found that they could use it, to such a degree that they almost became as good as the father. So, how could Fu Zi say that the dead man did not know how to live forever?"

"On Charms," *Lie Zi*

Note: *All the ancient rulers who believed in preposterous ideas such as living forever were stupid and brutal. Hu Zi's argument is reasonable, but his opinion that the teacher really did know how to live forever is ill-founded.*

36. Lao Zi Grasps the Tao

The founder of Taoism, Lao Zi, learned the Tao from Chang Zong. Chang Zong taught him nothing, but let him come to the truth by himself. Enlightened by the ancient Tao, Lao Zi sometimes looked up at trees and house ridges, and sometimes wandered through the mountains and by the rivers. When he looked at the sun, he thought of shadows. He finally realized that time could not stand still, and once it was gone it never returned. Shadows always followed the sunlight. Then he thought of the way the worthy lived: They always naturally followed others like the shadows following the sunlight. Like a cart carrying wood, the wood piled on it later is always on top of the wood that has been piled before. It was not the first, but it was on the top.

Lao Zi also realized that people must be self-aware: The clanging bell damaged itself with its tolling; the candle perished because it was able to burn and give off light; the leopard was hunted for its beautiful skin; men who were good at fighting perished at the hands of their adversaries; glib-tongued orators talked themselves into difficulties. Ability, Lao Zi concluded, brings trouble not help, and skill damages its possessor instead of preserving him. The Tao shuns brute courage, which cannot withstand mass resistance. The Tao avoids a peephole view, which prevents a person seeing widely. Brute courage and a peephole view are not the way of the Tao. Only when you regard your skill as nothing, Lao Zi realized, and are not limited by brute courage and a peepwhole view, can you grasp the Tao.

"Upper Virtue," *Wen Zi*

Note: *From natural phenomena, Lao Zi realized the way of doing nothing and following nature. Brute courage and a peephole view prevent one grasping the Tao. Only wise people who regard themselves as knowing nothing can realize the Tao. In the author's opinion, speechless education is the best and most natural way to approach the Tao.*

37. Abandoning the Name for the Fact

Huang Gong of the State of Qi (in the north of modern Shandong Province) was very modest. He had two beautiful daughters, but he always denied that they were beautiful, even going so far as to say that they were ugly. Gradually, his daughters became renowned for their ugliness. When they reached marriageable age, nobody ventured to make a proposal.

A widower from the State of Wei married one of Huang Gong's daughters, and found that she was very beautiful. Then to whomever he met, he said, "It is only Huang Gong's extreme modesty that gained his daughters a reputation for ugliness."

His words spread, and Huang Gong's daughters then became famous for their beauty. Young men flocked to ask for the hand of the unmarried daughter.

The daughters had inborn beauty; that was a fact. Huang Gong's modesty making his daughters notorious for ugliness only manifested itself in a name. A name comes from a fact, but it does not correspond to that fact. Only when the false name is destroyed, can the reality be revealed.

"The Great Way," *Yin Wen Zi*

Note: *This fable stresses that a name may not correspond to a fact, although it sometimes does. Only by going deep into it can one get to the truth of a matter.*

38. Lao Zi Visits His Sick Teacher

Shang Rong, Lao Zi's teacher, was seriously ill. Lao Zi hurried to comfort him.

"Sir, do you have any last words of wisdom for me?" Lao Zi asked.

"Yes, " replied Shang Rong, "when you go back to your hometown, you should alight from your carriage and enter on foot."

"Yes, sir. For I left home on foot, so I must return on foot."

"When you meet old people in your hometown, you should defer to them."

"Yes, sir. You taught me to respect my elders."

Shang Rong opened his mouth, and asked Lao Zi, "Can you find my tongue?"

"Yes, sir. Your tongue is still in your mouth."

"Look again. Can you find my teeth?" Shang Rong continued.

"No, sir. Your teeth are all gone."

Then Shang Rong asked Lao Zi: "Do you know the reason for that?"

"Yes, sir. You always say, 'Hardness is easy to break; softness is not.'" Lao Zi answered.

Shang Rong said, with satisfaction, "Remember that all things follow the way of hardness and softness."

"The Outer Chapters," *Shen Zi*

Note: *Lao Zi said, "Strength will be overcome; great trees will be felled. This is because hardness is weaker than softness." That is to say, weakness is better than sturdiness, softness is better than hardness. This was emphasized by Lao Zi again and again. This section on the tongue and the teeth is a vivid illustration of this idea.*

39. Xu Wugui Knows How to Judge Dogs and Horses

Guided by Ru Shang, the hermit Xu Wugui visited Marquis Wu of Wei (reigned 395-370 B.C.). Marquis Wu greeted him mockingly, "Sir, your life must be hard indeed in the wild mountain forests, as you have come to see me."

Xu Wugui said, "I have come to comfort you, Your Highness, not for you to comfort me! Now, if you persist in sating your sensual appetites and desires, and indulging your likes and dislikes, then you will weary yourself. So I have come to comfort you."

Marquis Wu looked blank and made no reply. A little later, Xu Wugui said, "I know how to judge dogs and horses. I can distinguish the best and the worst according to its looks. The lowest kind of dog grabs his food, gorges himself and then stops, having the habits of a fox; the medium sort of dog is always staring arrogantly at the sun, while the superior kind of dog appears to have forgotten himself. But my skill at judging horses goes far beyond this. I judge horses by whether they run in a straight line, or curve round holding the center, or turn as on a T-square, or circle like a compass. Such a horse as I describe is a fine horse for a nation, but not a fine horse for the world. A truly fine horse for the world looks anxious; he appears to lose his way, to forget himself. However, a horse like this suddenly prances along or rushes past, kicking up the dust, and no one knows where he has gone."

The Marquis laughed with delight.

Xu Wugui said goodbye, and left the court with Ru Shang. On the way back, Ru Shang asked him: "Sir, what did you discuss that made His Highness so pleased? When we discuss matters with him, we talk about weighty matters such as poetry, history, ritual and music, or the art of war. Countless people flatter him for making successful decisions. Yet in all our meetings I have never seen him smile. So what did you talk about?"

"I simply explained how I judged dogs and horses," said Xu Wugui.

"Really?"

"Have you never heard of the exile from Yue?" said Xu Wugui. "A few days after leaving there, he was delighted if he met someone from his country; a month after leaving, he jumped with joy if he saw something from Yue; a year after leaving, he was in an ecstasy of delight if he met someone from his country. The longer he was absent from his country, the fonder of it he became. Those people who retreat into the wild valleys where thick bushes block the path of even the weasels, and who have to struggle to move around, are delighted if they hear even the sound of a human footstep. How much more delighted will they be if they hear the sounds of their own brothers and family talking and laughing beside them. Perhaps it has been rather a long time since a man has sat and talked sincerely with your ruler!"

"Xu Wugui," *The Miscellaneous Chapters of Zhuang Zi*

Note: *People go against nature because of their self-confusions: desires, hatred and love, truth and falsehood, fame and gain. All these make life terribly fatiguing. Xu Wugui skillfully pointed that the best dog and horse forgot their bodies, so the best way is to treat the changes of all things in a detached manner.*

40. The Battling Snail Horns

In the 21st year of Duke Hui of Wei and the eighth year of Duke Wei of Qi (349 B.C.), the two rulers made an agreement not to attack each other. Seven years later, the Qi ruler broke the treaty and attacked Wei. The ruler of Wei was furious, and was planning to send an assassin to dispose of his Qi counterpart. Gongsun Yan, who was commander-in-chief, heard of this and considered it a shame, saying, "Sire, you have ten thousand chariots at your command; how could you stoop to using a paltry assassin? Give me 200,000 men, and I will destroy Qi and bring its ruler to you alive and bound hand and foot."

The minister Ji Zi then stepped forward, counselling caution: "We have been at great pains to construct peace between our two countries. Any rash action will render all our endeavors vain. I beg, Sire, that you do not heed the wild words of Gongsun Yan."

At this point another minister, Hua Zi, interjected with "Your Highness, the courses of action advocated by these two men are equally reckless. Calamity lies at the end of either road."

His master was puzzled. "What, in Heaven's name,

should I do, then?" he demanded.

Hua Zi advised the sovereign to follow the Tao, eschewing all personal inclinations. When the ruler still did not understand, Hua Zi brought the mystic Dai Jinren before him.

The first thing Dai Jinren did was to ask the monarch if he knew what a snail was. Mystified, the other replied, "Of course."

"Sire, do you know that there are two small kingdoms on the snail's head? The kingdom on its left horn is called Chushi and the one on its right horn is called Manshi. These kingdoms are constantly arguing over territory and fighting. The dead are heaped up in multitudes, with the defeated army fleeing—but within a few days, battle is rejoined."

When the duke displayed amused skepticism, the visitor changed his tack: "As for the four directions, and up and down, Sire, is there any limit to them?"

"No limit."

"That is correct. The hearts of those who know the Tao wander through unlimited realms, while their bodies stay in a country within the four seas and nine lands."

The ruler said, "Certainly."

"When the four seas and nine lands are compared to the unlimited universe, they are too small to calculate. Is that not right?"

"It is."

"The State of Wei is one of these countries, and in

the center of Wei is the capital, Daliang. And at the center of this capital is Your Majesty. Is there really any difference in importance between Wei and Qi and the two kingdoms on the snail's horns?"

The duke said, "There is not."

After Dai Jinren had departed, the duke said to Hui Zi: "That is a remarkable man, indeed."

Hui Zi said, "He is, Sire. If you blow on a flute or pipes, you get a pleasant sound. But if you blow on the pommel of your sword, you only get a wheezing noise. Yao and Shun are often praised. But if you talk about them in front of Dai Jinren, it sounds like a mere wheezing."

"Ze Yang," *The Miscellaneous Chapters of Zhuang Zi*

Note: *This story satirizes and strongly criticizes warlike rulers. Through greed, they fought for territory, at the cost of innocent lives. In the author's opinion, their strivings were no more important than the battles between the minute kingdoms on a snail's horns. From the viewpoint of the Tao, even a seemingly big thing like fighting among states is insignificant compared with the unlimited universe.*

41. Bo Ju Laments over a Corpse

Bo Ju, a disciple of Lao Zi, one day said to his master: "I would like to be allowed to wander the world."

Lao Zi said, "No! Everywhere under Heaven is the same."

Bo Ju begged again and again, and finally Lao Zi asked, "Where will you go first?"

"I will start with the State of Qi."

Lao Zi did not oppose his disciple's plan.

When Bo Ju arrived in Qi he saw the corpse of an executed criminal lying in the street. He hurried over and covered the body with his own cloak, wailing and lamenting all the while: "You unfortunate man! The powerful ones forbid stealing and murder, but they do not know that since praise and failure have been in this world suffering has accompanied them. When goods and fortunes are amassed, arguments spring up. Suffering, strife and poverty have brought you to this fate. The current world is worse than the ancient one. The rulers of ancient times saw their successes in terms of the people, and saw their failures in terms of themselves. They viewed the people as right and themselves as wrong. When the common people suffered, they would blame themselves. This is certainly not the case today. Today's rulers hide what should be done, and then blame the people when they don't understand; they never solve the problems, but punish those who cannot manage. They push people to the limit, and execute those who fall by the wayside. When people realize that they simply haven't the energy, they use pretence. When every day there is so much falsehood, how can the scholars and the people not become compromised? When strength is lacking, deceit is used; when knowledge is lacking, deception is used; when material goods are lacking, theft is used. But who really is to blame for these thefts?"

"Ze Yang," *The Miscellaneous Chapters of Zhuang Zi*

Note: *Praise and blame were defined by the ruling class, which devoted itself to the amassing of wealth, leaving the common people to scrabble for a living, and even resort to crime when all else failed. The author's aim in this anecdote is to point out the responsibility of society's rulers for the crimes committed by the common people.*

42. Fishing in the Wei River

In the late Shang Dynasty (11th century B.C.), the leader of the Zhou tribe, King Wen, toured Zang. There he saw an old man fishing in the Wei River. Strangely enough, the angler was using neither bait nor hook. King Wen realized that this must be an unusual person who did not care for loss or gain, and yearned for freedom. King Wen wanted to appoint this unusual man to govern the kingdom, but he was worried that such an action would upset his ministers, uncles and cousins. The next morning he summoned his court, and said, "Last night I dreamed that I saw a man of quality, bearded and with a dark complexion, riding a dappled horse, half of whose hooves were red. This man said to me: 'Pass your government to the worthy of Zang, and your people will escape calamity.'"

His ministers said with one voice: "It was the late king, Ji Li. He had a dark complexion and a beard. Also, he liked to ride a dappled horse with red hooves. It must have been him you dreamed of."

King Wen said, "Perhaps you are right. Let us ask the diviner."

But the ministers said, "It is the command of the

late king. Your Majesty should not doubt this. So there is no need for a diviner."

"Very well,"agreed the king.

So in due course King Wen handed over the government to the Old Man of Zang.

However, all the old order and regulations persisted unchanged, and no new laws were issued. Three years later King Wen toured his realm. He found that the chiefs of the departments no longer bragged about their positions, and that no one brought illegal weights or measures into the country. Everywhere there was peace and tranquillity. King Wen asked the Old Man of Zang what the reason for this state of affairs was, and the latter replied,

"Now the country enjoys peace and tranquillity, critics have nothing to do, so the mansions will be no need; the chiefs of departments sought no special honors, because they saw even the most mundane task as an honor. With the country unified the princes are now of one heart and one mind with Your Majesty. That's why the country is peaceful and in order."

Then King Wen asked him: "Could this government be extended to all the Earth?"

The Old Man of Zang looked confused and made no answer.

The next day he was nowhere to be found, and in fact was never heard of again.

The Old Man of Zang wanted to govern by doing nothing going against nature; his success depended on nature, not man. But others could not be relied upon to use his methods properly. Yan Hui, a disciple of Confucius, asked the sage about this, and the latter said, "Do not speak carelessly. King Wen let the Old Man of Zang govern his kingdom, but the Old Man did not attempt to influence others with his own ideas. The Old Man of Zang was proficient in the knowledge of the Tao; he guided people and followed their wishes. It was no surprise that King Wen used the dream to extract himself from his difficulty."

"Tian Zifang," *The Outer Chapters of Zhuang Zi*

Note: *The Old Man of Zang ran the country very well for three years. That meant that the way of doing nothing going against nature worked. When the king wanted the Old Man to extend his way to the whole Earth, the Old Man left without even saying goodbye. This indicated that the man, who had grasped the Tao, had no desire for power.*

43. The Yellow Emperor and the Horseherd

Four or five thousand years ago, the Yellow Emperor, in his quest for the Tao, went to see the hermit Da Kui on Mount Juzi (today's Mount Dakui). Fang Ming was the driver, and Chang Yu sat beside him. Zhang Ruo and Xi Peng guided the horses, and Kun Men and Hua Ji rode behind the carriage. When they eventually arrived in the wild region south of Mount Juzi, they lost their way. Coming upon a boy herding horses, they asked him: "Do you know how to get to Mount Juzi?"

"Certainly," said the boy.

"Do you know where Da Kui lives?"

"Of course."

The Yellow Emperor thought to himself, "What a remarkable lad! Not only does he know how to get to Mount Juzi, he also knows where Da Kui lives. He is perhaps an unusual person related to Da Kui. Why not ask him how to govern the world?"

When he made the offer, the boy replied, "Governing everything under Heaven is the same as what you and I are doing at the moment. Everything is done for self-cultivation. Doing nothing is nothing, nothing is nothing to do. What is so hard about that?

"When I was younger, I liked to wander within the confines of the six directions but my eyesight began to fail. A wise elderly gentleman told me, 'Climb up and ride in the carriage of the Sun and explore the wild region of Xiang Yang." Now my eyesight is better and I am able to wander beyond the borders of the six directions. Ruling everything under Heaven is just like this. So I need say no more."

The Yellow Emperor sighed, "Ruling everything under Heaven is neither your nor my problem. Even so, I would like to hear how to do it."

The lad did not answer. So the Yellow Emperor asked again. The boy said, "Governing everything under Heaven is surely rather like herding horses! Since you ask me again and again, let me tell you: Get rid of any evil member of a herd. Evil members of a herd do not fulfill their duties. People who govern the country must firstly govern themselves. To fulfill their duties, they must follow the nature. Or, like the evil horses, they will be harmful to others."

The Yellow Emperor bowed twice to him, called him his Heavenly Master, and departed.

"Xu Wugui," *The Miscellaneous Chapters of Zhuang Zi*

Note: *Running a country is the same as self-cultivation. The best way for self-cultivation is to do nothing going against nature.*

44. The Lover of Swords

King Wen (reigned 298-266 B.C.) of the State of Zhao (in the central part of modern Shanxi and the southwestern part of Hebei) loved swords. He kept over three thousand expert swordsmen. Day and night, they fought before him until the dead or wounded each year were more than a hundred. But the king never ceased to delight in watching them. Three years later, the country began to fall apart, and the other states began to plot its overthrow. Crown Prince Kui was distressed by this, and he discussed with his followers how to persuade the king to abandon his sword fighting entertainment. Someone recommended Zhuang Zi as their spokesman. The crown prince sent a messenger with a thousand pieces of gold to Zhuang Zi.

Zhuang Zi refused the gold, but returned with the messenger.

He went in to see the crown prince, and said, "Why did you send me a thousand pieces of gold?"

The crown prince replied, "I have heard, Sir, that you are an illustrious sage. The thousand pieces of gold was a gift for your services. However, you have refused to accept this, so what more dare I say?"

Zhuang Zi hesitated a while, and said, "I have heard that you wish me to try to persuade the king to give up his abiding passion. If in such an attempt I upset the king and fail to achieve what you hope for, then I might be executed. So what use would the gold be to me? If I could get him to give up his obsession with swordsmanship and fulfill your hopes, what is there in this whole kingdom of Zhao that I could not ask for and be given?"

The crown prince thought this reasonable, but then a worry occurred to him: "However the king will only see swordsmen. The swordsmen are all tousle-headed, with spiky beards. They wear loose caps held on with simple, rough straps, and robes that are cut short behind. They look about them fiercely and talk only of their sport. Now, if you seek an audience wearing your scholar's garb, it will be futile."

Zhuang Zi said, "Don't worry about that. I know swords; just give me a full swordsman's outfit."

Three days later Zhuang Zi outfitted as a fencing master, went with the crown prince to see the king. Entering the king's presence, Zhuang Zi did not kowtow. The king was displeased, saying, "What instruction have you for me, that you have persuaded the crown prince about beforehand?"

"I have heard that Your Majesty likes swords, and so I asked the Crown Prince to let me discuss swords with you."

"What use is your sword in combat?" the king asked.

"My sword can kill one person every ten paces, and even after a thousand miles it does not falter."

The king was impressed, and said, "Your sword must be all-conquering under Heaven!"

"A fine swordsman opens with a feint then gives ground, following up with a cut, stalling his opponent before he can react. I would like to show you my skills."

The king said, "Rest awhile in your quarters, Master, and await my command. I shall make arrangements for a contest, and call you."

The king spent the next seven days testing his swordsmen. More than 60 died or were severely wounded, leaving five or six who were selected to test Zhuang Zi's skill.

Then he called in Zhuang Zi and pointed to these swordsmen, saying, "This very day I shall pit you against these men to test your skill."

"I have longed for such an opportunity," said Zhuang Zi.

"Sir, what sort of sword will you choose, long or short?" asked the king.

"Any kind will do. But I have three swords of my own, any of which I can use if Your Majesty selects one for me."

The king said, "I would like to hear about these three swords."

Zhuang Zi replied, "I have the Sword of the Son of Heaven, the Sword of the Noble Prince and the Sword of the Commoner, Sire, which one would you choose?"

The king asked, "What is this Sword of the Son of Heaven?"

"The Sword of the Son of Heaven takes the Valley of Yen and the Stone Wall as its point, and the State of Qi and Mount Tai as its edge. The states of Jin and Wei are its ridge, Zhou and Song are its hilt, and Han and Wei its sheath. Other peoples, surrounded by barbarians, are included. It is wrapped in the four seasons. It can hold the Bohai Sea at a distance and Mount Tai close to it. It controls the world according to the Five Elements, and enacts what punishment and compassion dictate. It comes out in obedience to Yin and Yang; stands alert in spring and summer, when all things blossom with life; and goes into action in autumn and winter, when all things wither. When it is used, nothing can stop it. It can not be known how high and deep it points. Raised high, it cleaves the firmament; swung low, it cuts the very ground. Use this sword but once and all the rulers revert to obedience; all below Heaven submit. This is the Sword of the Son of Heaven."

The king asked, "What is the Sword of the Noble Prince?"

Zhuang Zi said, "The point of the Sword of the Noble Prince is sagacious and courageous people; its blade is people of integrity and sincerity; its ridge is people of worth and goodness; its hilt is people who are trustworthy and wise; its sheath is people who are brave and outstanding. This sword follows the nature of Heaven and Earth, and is made of the feelings of all forms of life. When it is thrust forward, it encounters nothing; when wielded high, it has nothing above it; when swung low, it has nothing below it; when swirled about, it finds nothing near it. Above, its guidance comes from Heaven, and it proceeds with the light of the sun, moon and stars; below, it is inspired by the square, stable nature of the earth, proceeding with the flow of the four seasons. In the middle lands it restores harmony to the people, and is in balance with the four directions. It is like hearing the crash of thunder. Within the four borders everyone obeys the laws and everyone attends to the orders of the ruler. This is the Sword of the Noble Prince."

"What is the Sword of the Commoner?" The king then asked.

"The Sword of the Commoner is used by those who are tousle-haired, with spiky beards, who fight each other whenever they meet. Raised high, it cuts through the neck; swung low, it slices into the liver and lungs. The people who use the Sword of the Commoner are no better than fighting cocks. They are useless to the state. Now you, the ruler, have the position of the Son of Heaven, but you make yourself unworthy by associating with the Sword of the Commoner. I feel sorry for Your Majesty."

The king suddenly saw the light, and took Zhuang Zi into his private hall, where the butler presented food, while the king paced the room, lost in morose ponderings.

Zhuang Zi comforted the king, saying, "Sire, please be seated and calm yourself. I have complied with your request. Now it is time for me to leave."

Following this, King Wen did not go out for three months, and all his swordsmen killed themselves, for they felt disgraced at losing the ruler's favor.

"The Lover of Swords," *The Miscellaneous Chapters of Zhuang Zi*

Note: *Pointing out the differences among the Sword of the Son of Heaven, the Sword of the Noble Prince and the Sword of the Commoner, Zhuang Zi persuaded King Wen of Zhao, who possessed the Sword of the Son of Heaven but was infatuated with the Sword of the Commoner, into giving up the latter and devoting himself to running the country.*

45. A Great Talent Takes Time to Mature

King Zhuang of the State of Chu (?-591 B.C., reigned 613-591 B.C.) did not issue a single order or attempt any policy during the first three years of his reign. Both his civil and military officials worried about the fate of their country.

One day his minister of war said to King Zhuang: "I have heard that there is a bird in the southern mountains that roosts for three years without either flying or singing. What do you think of that, Your Majesty?"

The king understood what his minister meant, and replied, "The bird does not fly, because it is strengthening its wings; it does not sing, in order to observe and learn the proper way of singing. If this bird were to take flight, it would puncture the blue sky and soar higher than Heaven; if it were to cry out, its cry would shake the world. Do you understand what I mean?!"

Half a year later the king began to rectify the laws of the state, execute venal officials and appoint talented people to high posts. The State of Chu grew more powerful day by day. It then conquered the State of Qi and the State of Jin. Following this, it made alliances with Song and other states, until it finally became the leader of all the states.

King Zhuang of Chu was not eager to show his abilities before the time was ripe. And so, he was finally able to achieve success. Just as a magnificent vessel takes a long time to complete, so too does outstanding talent take a long time to mature.

"Yu Lao," *Han Fei Zi*

Note: *In the first three years of his reign, King Zhuang studied the situation of his realm, prepared his policies and stored up his power. Therefore, when the time was ripe, he was able to embark on reform and actions which were inevitably crowned with success. This story stresses the importance of waiting for the right opportunity. He who skillfully bides his time and takes advantage of the propitious moment, will certainly succeed.*

46. Know Oneself

King Zhuang of the State of Chu wanted to attack the State of Yue (located in what is now northern Zhejiang and eastern Jiangsu), so he summoned a council of his ministers.

Du Zi said, "Your Majesty, why do you want to attack Yue?"

The king said, "Yue is in disorder and weak now. Now is the time to strike."

Du Zi shook his head, saying, "Sire, this is really a rash plan."

"What do you mean?" the king asked.

"A person's wisdom is like his eyes, which can look far into the distance, but cannot see his eyelashes. Chu's defeats at the hands of the states of Qin and Jin have lost it several hundred square miles of territory. That means that we are militarily weak. Zhuang Qiao's revolt caught us by surprise. That means that our political situation is chaotic. In my opinion, our situation is much worse than that of Yue. Now, is not Your Majesty's desire to attack Yue like a person's eyes?"

Thereupon the king abandoned his plan.

It is not difficult for people to know other things. But it is difficult for them to know themselves. Indeed, "Wisdom means knowing oneself!"

"Yu Lao," *Han Fei Zi*

Note: *Hearing Du Zi's analysis, King Zhuang of Chu gave up the idea of attacking Yue. He realized that he must first know himself. However, there are many people who, unlike King Zhuang, lack self-knowledge and end up running against a brick wall.*

47. Diving a Person's Thoughts from the Expression on His Face

Not long after Duke Xiang (reigned 627-621 B.C.) of the State of Jin came to power, he planned to extend his territory. One day he sent an emissary to King Jing of the Zhou Dynasty to inform him: "Our duke is ill. The oracle told him that his illness was caused by the god of Mt. Santu and that he should go there to ask for the god's blessings. I am here, Your Majesty, to beg you, on my master's behalf, to let my master go there by passing through your domain."

The king agreed and treated him with proper etiquette. After this, King Jing's minister Chang Hong said to Liu Kanggong, the son of Duke Ding, "There was a murderous look on the emissary of Jin's face. He must have come with ill intent. You'd better hurry back to your fief at Yanshi and make preparations against Jin's invasion."

Liu Kanggong thought it reasonable and returned to Yanshi to put his troops on the alert.

Having obtained King Jing of Zhou's consent, the Jin troops passed through the Central Plains and the Zhou capital, then veered to the strategic Yellow River ferry at Mengjin and conquered the three southern states of Liao, Ruan and Liang.

"Jing Yu," *Master Lu's Spring and Autumn Annals*

Note: *One's innermost thoughts can be told from the expression on his face. By seeing through Duke Xiang of Jin's ill intent from the look of his emissary, Chang Hong was able to persuade Liu Kanggong to take precautionary measures and keep his fief safe from conquest by the State of Jin.*

48. Getting Wei While Attacking Yuan

When Duke Wen of Jin was in exile, the ruler of Yuan in the Qinshui river valley was disrespectful to him. Later, after Duke Wen ended his exile and returned to Jin and succeeded to the throne, the ruler of Yuan refused to pledge his allegiance to the State of Jin. For this reason, Duke Wen of Jin decide to lead an expedition against Yuan.

Before the attack, the duke set a seven-day deadline for the war. But the attack met with stubborn resistance on the part of the Yuan's troops, so that seven days had passed and the Jin troops still couldn't win the battle. Then the duke ordered his troops to retreat to Jin.

Puzzled, one of his aides said:

"The Yuan troops are losing the battle. If we retreat now, all our previous efforts will be labor lost."

The duke disagreed, saying,

"Military orders can not be disobeyed. For a country, the most important thing is good faith. I will not get Yuan at the expense of the loss of good faith."

The next year, Duke Wen of Jin attacked Yuan

again. This time he vowed that he would not retreat if they could not occupy Yuan. Hearing of this, the ruler of Yuan surrendered.

When the ruler of the neighboring state, Wei, heard about that, he voluntarily surrendered to Jin.

"Wei Yu," *Master Lu's Spring and Autumn Annals*

Note: *This fable indicates that a ruler must keep good faith if he wants to realize his goal.*

49. Foresight and Premonition

Everything under Heaven has relations of advantage and disadvantage to other things. For those who are born and live in peace with each other, advantages appear; for those who harm each other, disadvantages appear. These kinds of things are numberless. The development of things is determined by man, and man is determined by his desires. Unlimited desires lead to unlimited minds; unlimited minds lead to unimaginable actions. The sages are never confused and have foresight, for they can observe signs and the appearance of things.

When the master strategist Wu Qi was the governor of Xihe Prefecture in the State of Wei the neighboring State of Qin dared not try to extend its territory east of the Yellow River. Certain of his enemies, led by Wang Cuo, maligned and slandered Wu Qi before Marquis Wu of Wei (reigned 395-370 B.C.). The marquis then summoned him back to the capital.

When Wu Qi's carriage left the main gate of Xihe, he alighted, and climbed a hill. There, he looked down on the river and wept.

His servant enquired, "Sir, you have always harbored lofty ambitions, and considered ordinary matters as of no more importance than a discarded ragged shoe. Why are you so sad today?"

Wu Qi replied, "If our ruler really knew me and let me give full play to my skill and wisdom, Qin would perish, while Xihe would be the basis for Wei to become the strongest among all the states. But the marquis does not know me and believes villains' words. Xihe will be seized by Qin in the near future and Wei will wither, all because it has lost Xihe."

Persecuted back in the capital, Wu Qi took refuge in the State of Chu. Not long after, Xihe was occupied by Qin. Wei began its process of decline, and Qin became more powerful day by day. Thus, events turned out as Wu Qi had predicted.

"Observing Signs," *Master Lu's Spring and Autumn Annals*

Note: *This story is a lesson to rulers to examine signs and symptoms meticulously so as to grasp the essence of situations. The rise and fall of a country may depend upon how accurately this is done.*

50. The Muddle-Headed King and the the Crafty Minister

In the Spring and Autumn Period, King Ping of Chu (reigned 528-516 B.C.), had a crafty and fawning minister named Fei Wuji. The latter was jealous of the crown prince, Jian, who he considered stood between him and the king.

When the crown prince married a beautiful woman from the State of Qin, Fei Wuji trapped the king into having relations with her. As a consequence, father and son became estranged.

In order to separate the king and his eldest son even further, Fei Wuji persuaded his master to send the crown prince to the border city of Chengfu, citing a purported threat from Chu's neighbor, the State of Jin. Chengfu, he argued, being in the north, was the very place for the crown prince to solicit the aid of the states of Song, Zheng, Lu and Wei against Jin, which lay to the north of Chu.

The following year Fei Wuji reported to the king that the crown prince was plotting a rebellion, as he still nurtured resentment against his father. The crown prince's accomplice, according to Fei Wuji, was the governor of Chengfu, Wu She. The king thereupon had Wu She put to death, and the crown prince fled to another state.

Fei Wuji next turned his sights on the popular minister Qie Wan. He passed a message to the son of the prime minister, to the effect that Qie Wan had invited him and his father to a banquet. He then informed Qie Wan that he should expect a visit from the prime minister.

Qie Wan was nonplussed. "Why should the prime minister deign to pay a visit to a nonentity like myself?" he asked. "And how shall I please him when he comes?"

Fei Wuji replied, "The prime minister is a connoisseur of fine weapons. Put all your best swords and pikes on display inside the door; I am sure that he will be delighted when he sees them."

When the day of the feast arrived, Fei Wuji, having ascertained that Qie Wan had stocked the weapons in the hallway, rushed to the prime minister's residence and pretended to warn him of a plot against his life. "I myself saw the weapons Qie Wan has prepared to slay you with the moment you set foot in his house," he gasped. "Forgive me for nearly leading you into a trap." The prime minister thereupon sent one of his men to ascertain the truth of this claim, and when the man reported that weapons had in fact been stacked in the portico of Qie Wan's mansion, immediately gave orders that the latter be put ot death.

But Fei Wuji's scheming had not escaped the notice of the king's great-grandson Shen Yinshu, who had made a careful note of the crafty official's devious plots.

Shen explained Fei's strategy to the prime minister, and the latter lost no time in ordering the execution of Fei Wuji and the whole of his clan.

"Act with Caution," *Master Lu's Spring and Autumn Annals*

Note: *The author emphasizes that people should act according to the principles of morality and justice, and take people of high morality as their models. He who acts according to the principles of morality and justice can safeguard both the country and himself; he who chases after private interest, ignoring morality and justice, will get nothing. Fei Wuji's self-interest brought about his death. King Ping of Chu was gullible and brutal, and so he was hated by his people long after his death.*

51. Repenting at the Point of Death

The ruler of the State of Wu, Fu Chai (reigned 514-496 B.C.), was planning to attack the State of Qi. Wu Zixu, one of his close advisors, admonished him thus: "Sire, Qi is a land where the customs and speech are different from those of Wu. If we succeed in subduing Qi we will have great difficulty ruling and absorbing its people. Our neighbor, the State of Yue, on the other hand, shares with us both customs and language. This means that Yue itself could conquer and swallow us up as easily as we could do the same to them. It behooves us, therefore, to launch a pre-emptive strike on Yue before turning our attention to our old rival Qi."

Court Steward Pi objected, saying, "Your Majesty would be unwise to heed this advice. Yue is insignificant in the context of the great powers; its absorption would do little to enhance Your Lordship's might and prestige among the states. The swift conquest of Qi would force the capitulation of Jin and project the dominance of your realm across the Central Plains."

Fu Chai was swayed by these words, and ordered a general mobilization for a campaign against Qi.

Wu Zixu angered his master at this point by saying, "I venture to predict, Sire, that victory over Qi will result in annihilation for our state."

Fu Chai did in fact defeat Qi, and, upon his return, ordered that Wu Zixu be put to death. The latter said, "I beg, Sire, that you will at least preserve one of my eyes, wherewith I may some day see the destruction of the State of Wu by Yue." With this, he cut his own throat and died on the spot. The ruler, in contempt, had both of Wu Zixu's eyes gouged out and his dead body hung on the eastern gate of the capital (facing Yue), saying, "Now you will be able to see the Yue forces advancing on Wu—if they ever come!"

Just over a decade later, the fortunes of Yue revived, and it became a powerful state once more. It occupied the capital of Wu, destroyed Fu Chai's ancestors' temple and captured Fu Chai alive. Before committing suicide, Fu Chai regretted that he had not listened to Wu Zixu, saying, "If the shades in the nether world know everything that goes on here on earth, how can I face Zixu when we meet?"

The wise are able to analyze the times and judge the occasion. The stupid refuse to listen to warnings and advice, with the result that trouble comes upon them; and by that time it is too late.

"Zhi Hua," *Master Lu's Spring and Autumn Annals*

Note: *Fu Chai and his country perished because he did not grasp the reality of change. The author believes that a ruler should listen to blunt advice with an open mind in order to understand the natural trend of things in advance, and take the necessary measures against disaster as early as possible.*

52. Ren Zuo Speaks Bluntly

Marquis Wen of Wei (reigned 445-396 B.C.) gave a banquet for his officials, and asked them their opinions of himself. The first few all vied with each other in heaping praise on their sovereign, lauding his benevolence, wisdom, and so on to the skies. But when it came to the turn of Ren Zuo, a guest of the ruler, he said, "Your Majesty is not a good ruler. When you overran the State of Zhongshan, your brother made the biggest contribution to that victory; yet you granted its territory to your son. That was not the act of a good ruler."

Hearing this, everyone was horrified, and the marquis' face turned as black as thunder. Ren Zuo thereupon hurriedly left.

Then it was Zhai Huang's turn to give his opinion. He said, "It seems to me that Your Majesty is wise and able. I have heard that a wise and able ruler dare officials speak bluntly. Just now, Ren Zuo spoke bluntly, and that proves that Your Majesty is wise and able."

The marquis realized the truth of this, and urged Zhai Huang: "Please get him to return."

Zhai Huang said, "Certainly. Faithful officials never seek to avoid the consequences of their honest advice, so Ren Zuo will not have gone far, I expect."

Going out of the hall, Zhai Huang found Ren Zuo waiting just outside the door. As he accompanied Zhai Huang back into the hall, Ren Zuo was met by the marquis himself, who declared that Ren Zuo would be his lifetime guest.

"Know Yourself," *Master Lu's Spring and Autumn Annals*

Note: *It is essential for a ruler to be aware of his own mistakes. The author advises rulers to listen to honest criticism from loyal people.*

53. Winning the People's Confidence

General Wu Qi was appointed by Marquis Wen of Wei to bring the newly-conquered Xihe region under control. The first thing he did was to erect a stone column outside the main gate of Xihe City. He then announced, "Whoever can uproot the column and bring it to my headquarters will be offered a ministerial post."

As it was a criminal offence to uproot such a pillar, at first nobody dared to try, not trusting Wu Qi's words. But finally one man plucked up courage, uprooted the pillar and carried it to Wu Qi's headquarters. Thereupon, he did indeed receive a ministerial post.

Wu Qi then ordered another pillar to be erected at the same gate and made the same offer as before. People swarmed forward to uproot the pillar, but this time it was planted too solidly for anyone to uproot it. In this way, Wu Qi won the confidence of the people of Xihe.

"Mindful of Small Things," *Master Lu's Spring and Autumn Annals*

Note: *Wu Qi knew that winning the confidence of the people was the first step he would have to take if he wanted his orders obeyed.*

54. If the Lips Are Gone, the Teeth Will Be Cold

King Ai of Jin sent General Zhi Boyao to attack the State of Zhao at the head of an army composed of the allied forces of Jin, Wei and Han.

After suffering a series of defeats, Xiang Zi (reigned 475-425 B.C.), the ruler of Zhao, confided in his top advisor, Zhang Mengtan, that his forces were at the end of their tether. Zhang said, "The only way out is to split Jin from its allies."

Given permission to make such an attempt, Zhang went secretly to the enemy camp and there met the rulers of Wei and Han. He said to them: "Have you ever heard the proverb, 'If the lips are gone, the teeth will be cold'? The lips and teeth are intimately connected with each other. If the lips are gone, the teeth remain, but without protection, they will be attacked by the cold. Zhao is like the lips which protect Wei and Han from the cold wind from Jin. Now, you and Zhi Boyao are attacking us together, if Zhi Boyao occupies Zhao, he will sooner or later turn his attention to your states. If you don't act soon, Zhao will fall and you will be doomed."

The rulers of Wei and Han were convinced by this vivid argument, and together with Zhang Mengtan hatched a plot to bring about the downfall of Jin.

One dark night, troops from Zhao breached the dykes on a nearby river in such a manner that part of the Jin camp was threatened by the floodwaters. Just as large numbers of Jin troops were busy trying to mend the dykes, their erstwhile allies from Wei and Han turned on them, assisted by an all-out attack by the Zhao forces. Zhi Boyao's men were utterly routed, and the result was that the three victorious states divided the territory of Jin between them.

"Lessons from the Human World," *Huai Nan Zi*

Note: *Zhang Mengtan used his ingenuity and diplomatic skill to save his country from destruction. His clever simile has passed into common usage to mean a relationship of absolute dependence.*

55. The Oxherd Who Met Good Fortune

Ning Yue from the State of Wei was a wise and talented man who cherished high ambitions. But being a poor common man, he could get nobody to recommend him for an official post. He greatly admired Duke Huan of the neighboring State of Qi (reigned 685-643 B.C.) and wanted to assist him. So he joined a caravan of merchants who were journeying to Linzi, the capital of Qi, as an oxherd. For weeks, he stayed in the merchants' camp outside the city walls, with no way of gaining an audience with the duke.

Then one night the city gate opened, and Duke Huan emerged in the midst of a splendid torchlight procession. Seeing the magnificence of the scene, Ning Yue sighed at the hopelessness of his ambitions, and launched into a sad song. The duke heard the song and was deeply moved by it. He thereupon ordered that the singer be brought to entertain him at the court.

When Ning Yue was presented to him, Duke Huan soon realized that he was not only a talented singer, but was also well versed in statecraft. He straightaway appointed Ning Yue to a ministerial post.

There was outrage and consternation at this among the other court officials, who protested that Ning Yue was not even a native of the State of Qi, and nothing was known about his background.

But the ruler said, "If I enquire into his background, I am sure to find some skeleton or other in his closet. That would cloud my judgment; I prefer to concentrate on using Ning Yue's talents to benefit our state."

"Taoist Teachings," *Huai Nan Zi*

Note: *Duke Huan of Qi refused to enquire about Ning Yue's past, for he feared to lose his talent if some weak points were discovered. The way he treated the talented is praiseworthy.*

56. Bide One's Time Before One Acts

The last ruler of the Shang Dynasty (16th-11th centuries B.C.), Di Xin, has gone down throughout Chinese history as the epitome of tyranny. As his people grew more restless under his oppressive rule, they increasingly looked upon Ji Chang, leader of the Zhou tribe, which was a tributary of Shang, as a model leader. Ji Chang's acts of benevolence won him a fine reputation far and wide, and Di Xin feared that his people might overthrow him and put Ji Chang on his throne.

Unable by nature to vie with Ji Chang in benevolent deeds, Di Xin had him seized and thrown into prison.

Knowing the ruler's greedy disposition, Ji Chang's steward delivered lavish presents to the palace, and finally got his master released.

Ji Chang's advisors urged him to raise an army and topple the tyrant, but Ji Chang preferred to bide his time, and strike when his enemy was least prepared. Therefore, he pretended to immerse himself in idleness and pleasure. When the Shang ruler's spies reported that Ji Chang had apparently abandoned all political ambitions and was neglecting his people, Di Xin was convinced that Ji Chang was no longer a threat to him. Little did he know that Ji Chang was busy making secret preparations for an armed revolt.

Just as Di Xin's dissipation and brutality reached a crescendo, Ji Chang led the long-suffering subjects of Shang in an uprising which ousted the hated Di Xin. Ji Chang then came to the throne as the hallowed King Wen, founder of the Zhou Dynasty (11th century-221 B.C.).

"Taoist Teachings," *Huai Nan Zi*

Note: *Ji Chang concealed his ambition and built up his strength secretly, and at the crucial moment overthrew the tyrant of the Shang Dynasty. The author points out the importance of biding one's time and striking while the iron is hot.*

57. Jian Shu Wails for the Troops

Duke Mu of Qin (r. 659-621 B.C.) was preparing to attack Zheng. Jian Shu objected, saying, "Your preparations for this campaign, Sire, are woefully inadequate. Our forces must trudge through the territories of several states before they reach Zheng; both men and horses will be exhausted, and the supply lines will be too long. The keys to victory are high morale and adequate supplies. I fear that neither of these will be forthcoming. I therefore beg Your Majesty to call off this rash expedition."

The duke ignored this plea, and set forth at the head of his army to attack Zheng. As he did so he passed Jian Shu seated by the wayside. He was dressed in mourning and wailing for the troops, who he considered were marching to their destruction.

Marching toward Zheng, the Qin troops passed through the Central Plains, which were under the control of the King of Zhou.

It so happened that a dealer in oxen from the State of Zheng was in those parts on business. He slaughtered 12 of his beasts and gave a feast for the Qin army, saying that is was a gift from Duke Wen of Zheng.

The commander of the Qin troops wondered, "We have come from thousands of leagues away, and yet the ruler of Zheng must have known of our march long ago. This surely means that Zheng must have made adequate preparations against the invasion." So thinking, the Qin commander called off the march.

However, because of his war preparations, Duke Mu had neglected to go and pay his condolences at the court of his ally, the State of Jin, whose ruler had just died. This angered the successor to the throne, and he launched a surprise attack on the Qin army. The result was a defeat for the Qin side. In addition, because of his rash action, Duke Mu on the one hand lost an ally, and on the other failed to inflict any damage on his enemy, the State of Zheng.

Lao Zi said: The Tao cannot be known, but the way of directing a military operation can be spoken out. The Tao appreciates knowing without speaking; the Tao eschews pretending to know when not knowing. Rash and unconsidered action must be avoided when commanding troops. Jian Shu knew that well.

"Taoist Teachings," *Huai Nan Zi*

Note: *Lao Zi had pointed out that the way of war was profound and mysterious, and rash and unconsidered action must be avoided. Jian Shu understood this. So when Duke Mu went heedlessly ahead with his expedition against Zheng, brushing aside the warning of Jian Shu he came to grief.*

58. A Long-Range Plan or a Temporary Expedient

In 632 B.C. Duke Wen of Jin, Chong Er, was challenged by the State of Chu to a fight at Chengpu (southwest of modern Fanxian County, Henan). Not sure of winning the upcoming battle, Chong Er went to ask the advice of his uncle, Jiu Fan.

Jiu Fan said, "As the saying goes, 'Nothing is too deceitful in war.' So, Sire, you can use deceit."

Then, the duke went to consult his advisor, Yong Ji., who said,

"War is like hunting. If you burn the forest, you can catch many beasts, but you will catch no more beasts in the future. For this battle with Chu, you may win a signal victory by deceitful means, but, you cannot do the same in the future. Sire, you'd better employ open and aboveboard ways."

The duke turned down his proposal in favor of Jiu Fan's and, as a result, put the Chu troops to rout.

After the war, when the duke awarded his generals and soldiers, he gave first place to Yong Ji instead of Jiu Fan. Asked why, the duke replied, "It's true I owe this victory to Jiu Fan's suggestion. His suggestion, however, leads to only a temporary solution. What Yong Ji suggested seemingly has nothing to do with the past battle, but it is a long-range plan. How can I think of a long-range plan after a temporary expedient?"

"Lessons from the Human World," *Huai Nan Zi*

Note: *In this story, the author suggests that planning things on a long-term basis is more important than a plan that works only as an expedient.*

59. Ximen Bao's Administration

Ximen Bao was appointed governor of the district of Ye by Marquis Wen (reigned 445-396 B.C.) of the State of Wei. Before long, there was no grain in the storehouses, no money in the treasury, and no weapons in the armory. At the same time, the local officials came and went as they pleased, and paid no attention to their duties. Eventually, complaints about Ximen Bao reached Marquis Wen. The marquis was puzzled, and paid a visit to Ye himself to investigate the situation. When he demanded of Ximen Bao how affairs had managed to reach such a sorry state, the latter replied, "Mediocre governors put on a show of power and wealth by enforcing strict discipline on the people and wringing grain from them. But this is just hollow posturing. I have made the district of Ye truly powerful and wealthy by storing all prosperity and strength among the people. If you do not believe me, mount with me the drum tower."

Standing atop the drum tower, the puzzled marquis watched as Ximen Bao struck the signal drum once. Before the echo of the drumbeat had died away, people swarmed into the streets, clad in armor and bearing glittering weapons. Ximen Bao struck the drum a second time, whereupon cartloads of grain rumbled into the city.

Marquis Wen was astonished and delighted. He asked Ximen Bao how he had managed to make the people of Ye so loyal. The other replied, "The relationship of loyalty is consolidated through a long and natural course of trust and harmony. It is impossible to re-establish once broken. Now, the state of Yan often harasses our eight cities. I would like to attack Yan and recover our lost territories, now that the people of Ye are solidly behind me."

The marquis agreed. Ximen Bao then attacked Yan, and not long afterward regained Wei's lost territories.

"Lessons from the Human World," *Huai Nan Zi*

Note: *Following a policy of doing nothing against nature, Ximen Bao made Ye strong and prosperous. As a consequence, he was able to defeat Yan and recover Wei's lost territories.*

60. Demanding the Wayward Ox

When a pro-Jin usurper seized the throne of the State of Chen following the death of Duke Ling (reigned 613-599 B.C.), Duke Zhuang of Chu—a rival of the State of Jin—intervened. Slaying the usurper, Duke Zhuang left his eldest son to administer Chen.

The senior official of Chu, Shen Shushi, was in the State of Qi as an envoy at that time. When he returned and heard what his sovereign had done, he went into seclusion.

Duke Zhuang sent for Shen Shushi and told him: "The State of Chen was in disarray. I intervened to punish rebellion, but you seem to disapprove. Why?"

In reply, Shen Shushi invented a parable, saying, "A man's ox went astray and trampled his neighbor's corn. The neighbor demanded the ox as compensation for his ruined crops. Do you think that would have been a fair price to pay for the damage? The turmoil in Chen was, I am sure, alarming. And your intervention was most timely. But you placed your son at the helm of state affairs in Chen, and this is viewed by the other states as virtual annexation. In other words, Your Majesty has sequestered the ox even before it began to trample your corn!"

Thinking Shen Shushi was right, Duke Zhuang recalled his son from Chen, and this won the rulers of other states' respect for him.

"Lessons from the Human World," *Huai Nan Zi*

Note: *Although Duke Zhuang had good intentions, his actions were misinterpreted by his neighbors. Shen Shushi proferred a timely warning.*

61. King Xuan's Predilections

King Xuan of Qi (reigned 319-301 B.C.) asked his counsellor Chunyu Kun: "What do you think my predilections are?"

Chunyu Kun replied, "The ancient kings loved four things; of these, Sire, you love three."

The king urged him to explain.

"The ancient kings," pursued the advisor, "were fond of fine horses—as you are. They enjoyed rare delicacies of the table—as you do. They exulted in the company of beautiful women—as you do. But, unlike you, the ancient kings admired men of talent."

The king protested, "I too admire men of talent. It is just that there are no men of talent in our country at present. That is why there are none in my service."

Chunyu Kun said, "The magnificent steeds of ancient times, like Hualiu and Qiji, I grant you, are not to be found nowadays. Yet Your Majesty still picks fine horses for your stables. The fabled delicacies of the past, like leopard and elephant embryo, no longer grace the banquet table. Yet Your Majesty still dines on sumptuous dishes. No maid these days can match the legendary beauties Mao Qiang and Xi Shi. Yet

Your Majesty's harem never lacks dazzling damsels. May I venture to suggest that your court lacks talented men, not because such people do not exist but because they avoid coming to your attention."

At this, the king was dumbfounded.

"Respect the Virtuous," *Garden of Anecdotes*

Note: *Chunyu Kun pointed out that King Xuan of Qi had no trouble picking fine horses, delicious food and beauties because these things were brought to the king's notice. If men of talent hid themselves from him, the reason must be that he was not worthy of their service.*

62. The Poor's Pride

After occupying the State of Zhongshan (today's Dingxian County, Hebei), Marquis Wen of Wei started his journey home. Tian Zifang, a disciple of Zi Gong, a pupil of Confucius, brought up the rear. When the crown prince, Ji, saw him he got off his carriage and hurriedly went up to Tian Zifang. Tian Zifang remained in his carriage and said to him,

"Please tell the marquis to wait for me at court."

Displeased, the prince asked him, "Can you tell me who are more arrogant, the poor or the rich?"

Tian Zifang replied, "The poor, of course. How can a rich man afford to be arrogant? If the ruler of a state is arrogant, he will lose his country. So far I've not seen such rulers. If a minister is arrogant, he will lose his fief. So far I've not seen such ministers. A poor man has nothing to worry about or to lose. If he is displeased with someone, off he will go without any misgiving about loss of this or that. So, I think the poor can afford to be arrogant, while the rich can not."

When the crown prince told Marquis Wen what Tian Zifang had said, the marquis, instead of being offended, nodded with approval.

"Respect the Virtuous," *Garden of Anecdotes*

Note: *In this story, the author points out that only when a ruler treats talented people with courtesy, can his cause be prosperous.*

63. A Sobering Visitor

In the Spring and Autumn Period, Sun Shu'ao was appointed prime minister by King Zhuang of Chu. Immediately, crowds of well-wishers descended on his mansion. After receiving the congratulations and expressions of praise from a number of them, Sun Shu'ao was surprised to see an old man wearing mourning garb and with a solemn expression on his face advancing toward him.

He questioned the old man as follows: "Today people have come from far and wide to congratulate me on my good fortune. You alone, sir, appear to be saddened by it. You must have some sobering message for me."

The old man said, "What I want to tell you is that the common people will shun you if you are arrogant to them, and the ruler will detest you if you act recklessly on your own authority. Moreover, if you are not content with your lot, disaster may come at any time."

Sun Shu'ao said, "I completely accept what you say, and I would like to learn more."

The old man continued, "Although you are a

high-ranking official, you should listen to the views of the common people. You should be more careful and stricter as you become promoted. Finally, you must never make an inappropriate request. Remember these three points, and the State of Chu will be well ruled."

"Jing Shen," *Garden of Anecdotes*

Note: *Sun Shu'ao's promotion deserved to be celebrated, but the old man came with a grave message. Sun Shu'ao was not angry, but respectfully asked for the old man's instruction. The author here stresses the reality of increased responsibility behind the facade of celebration.*

64. Longevity, Wealth and Honor

King Xuan of Qi went hunting in Sheshan County. Thirteen local elders came to pay their respects to him. The king was pleased, and ordered his servants, "Excuse them from land taxes."

The old men all thanked him, with the exception of one named Lu Qiu. The king noticed this, and said, "Well, if that does not satisfy all of you, I excuse you and your families from corvee labor."

Again, all the old men except Lu Qiu humbly thanked him.

Dismissing the others, King Xuan said to Lu Qiu: "Today, I wanted to reward you by excusing you from land taxes. Everyone except you thanked me. Thinking that that was not enough, I then excused you from corvee labor. Again, everyone except you thanked me. Would you mind telling me the reason for this odd behavior?"

Lu Qiu replied, "We hoped to obtain longevity, wealth and honor from you."

The king said, "One's life span is determined by Heaven; I can do nothing about it. The state granary is overflowing, but that grain is to be used for disasters;

I can not give it to you. High rank is reserved for those with talent; I can not elevate you."

Lu Qiu said, "Your Majesty misunderstood. What I hope is that Your Majesty will appoint cultured and virtuous people as officials. If they act according to the law and ensure our lives are peaceful, we can live longer. If throughout the year the common people are allowed to go about their work without interference, we can be richer. If Your Majesty popularizes education, then youth will respect their elders, and their elders will respect the aged. In this way, I can be eminent. Today, Your Majesty rewarded us by excusing us from taxes. But this may deplete the storehouses. Excusing people from corvee labor may influence the state's welfare. This is not what we want."

The king was delighted, and appointed Lu Qiu his senior minister on the spot.

"Shan Shuo," *Garden of Anecdotes*

Note: *Lu Qiu pointed out that rewards and dispensations were not what the people wanted and were not in accord with the state's fundamental interests. Clean politics, fair regulations and laws and the promotion of virtue were the fundamental interests of the state and the people.*

65. Ever-New Clothes, Ever-Full Granary

Zhang Lu became prime minister of the State of Qin in 266 B.C. on the strength of a recommendation by Lord Meng Chang of his home state, Wei. One day he called on Lord Meng Chang, and asked, "Do you know how to ensure that your clothes will always be new and your granary always full?"

When Meng Chang admitted his bafflement and asked him to explain further, Zhang Lu said, "By recommending other talented people when you yourself are in a high position and by giving relief to the poor when you are rich."

Meng Chang was pleased, and the next day sent Zhang Lu presents of gold and silk, which the latter refused. When Meng Chang asked him why he had refused the gifts, Zhang Lu said, "Simply giving away your wealth will not earn you the means wherewith to keep your clothes ever new and your granary ever full. However, if you were to write a letter of recommendation for me to the ruler of Qin, who knows but that you may be assured of blessings in the future?"

Meng Chang wrote the letter, which gained Zhang

Lu a lucrative post in Qin.

In his new and influential position, Zhang Lu lost no time in putting a good word in the ruler of Qin's ear about Meng Chang. As a consequence, Meng Chang found his services much in demand, and costly presents constantly arriving at his door.

"Shan Shuo," *Garden of Anecdotes*

Note: *The author reminds the reader that high rank and wealth are not in themselves guarantees of honor and riches; one must constantly help others of talent and succor the poor.*

66. Yan Zi Snickers at Duke Jing

Duke Jing of Qi (reigned 547-490 B.C.) went sightseeing on Mt. Niushan, where, when he saw a panoramic view of his beautiful capital city, he lamented,

"How beautiful my country is! Why should everyone have died and left this country?"

On hearing this, his ministers Shi Kong and Liang Qiuju said through their tears:

"We have fared much worse than Your Highness. Even so, we do not want to die. Why should you, Sire, think of death?"

At this, another minister Yan Zi, who was standing some distance from the three, snickered. Puzzled, the duke asked Yan Zi:

"Just now I felt very sad, and Shi Kong and Liang Qiuju felt sad too. Why is it that you alone laughed?"

Yan Zi replied, "If virtuous dukes like Tai and Huan and brave dukes like Zhuang and Ling were not dead and remained in their positions, Your Highness would now be a farmer working behind the plough. A ruler of a nation has a busy work schedule, is there any time for him to think of death? Your Highness can peacefully succeed to the throne, because your predecessors have left this world one by one. Your crying for this, therefore, is against the principle of benevolence, and those who cried together with you are mere sycophants. I snickered at an unbenevolent ruler and his obsequious ministers."

The duke felt ashamed and made himself and the two officials each drink two cups of wine as a forfeit.

"Li Ming," *Lie Zi*

Note: *This story satirizes rulers who fondly hope always to enjoy wealth and honor and tilts at those who seek to curry favor with them by chiming in with whatever they say.*

67. Two Views of Politics

Gongsun Qiao (?-522 B.C.), also named Zi Chan, was the prime minister of the State of Zheng. Under his administration, the state was well run and the good obeyed him while the bad and other states feared him.

Zi Chan had an elder brother named Gongsun Chao, and a younger brother named Gongsun Mu. Gongsun Chao loved wine, while Gongsun Mu loved women.

Gongsun Chao's house was filled with choice wines of every description. He spent his days carousing, caring nothing for either his family or the state.

Meanwhile, Gongsun Mu was equally oblivious to the cares of the world, lounging day in and day out in his harem.

Zi Chan was distressed at this state of affairs, so he sought the advice of the sagely Deng Xi.

"Reverend sir," he said, "the ancients taught that self-cultivation would spread its benignity first to one's immediate family, and later to the state. However, in my case, although I have managed to bring peace and order to the state, yet my own brothers are steeped in dissipation. What should I say to them to make them see the error of their ways?"

Deng Xi said, "You should point out to them the importance of a life dedicated to service and the folly of a life devoted to pleasure."

Zi Chan thereupon went to see his brothers and urged them to turn over a new leaf. But the pair were scornful of his admonitions. "Life is short, while death is long," they reminded him. "Spending one's time in the harried pursuit of riches and honor is equivalent to embracing death as far as we are concerned. We came not a whit for honor and reputation; they cannot stand in the way of our enjoying life."

Dispirited, Zi Chan returned to his mentor Deng Xi, and related to him the encounter with his brothers. Deng Xi's only comment was: "Then the fact that the State of Zheng is well governed must be attributed to some accident. If they are the wise ones, you yourself have no merit!"

"Yang Zhu," *Lie Zi*

Note: *Deng Xi's ambiguous concluding remark shows a typical Taoist attitude to worldly affairs. Is he praising the dissolute brothers or comforting Zi Chan? Or is he merely hinting that all striving, whether for sensuous pleasure or fame and fortune, goes against nature and is doomed to frustration?*

68. Espying Robbers

Once upon a time, the State of Jin was plagued by robbers. The Marquis of Jin was worried about this, until a man called Qie Yong said he could tell if a man was a robber just by looking at him. The marquis let him pick out the people he thought were robbers from among the crowds in the streets and markets. It turned out that he was right every time, and hundreds of robbers were arrested.

The ruler was happy and said to Zhao Wenzi: "Only one Qie Yong is enough. Soon our state will be free from the scourge of robbers."

But Zhao Wenzi said, "Your Majesty, in my opinion, Qie Yong will not die a natural death."

Sure enough, before long those robbers who remained hatched a plot, and assassinated Qie Yong.

The marquis was shocked. He at once called Zhao Wenzi and said to him, "Sir, what you predicted really happened. Qie Yong was killed by robbers. How can I deal with this situation?"

Zhao Wenzi said, "An ancient saying goes, 'He who can see fishes in deep water is inauspicious; he who can espy hidden people may bring disaster.' If you want to rid the state of robbers once and for all, you should select worthy men to serve you. They will purify the government, educate the people in the way of virtue, and give everyone a sense of shame. Who then will want to be a robber?"

Accepting Zhao Wenzi's suggestion, the ruler appointed Sui Hui to administer the country. Before long robbers were leaving Jin in droves, and fleeing westward to the State of Qin.

"On Charms," *Lie Zi*

Note: *The only sure way to eradicate moral turpitude is by educating the people in righteousness. Tricks like that used by Qie Yong may work for a while, but they are not the basic solution to any problem.*

69. Worried by Victory

Zhao Xiangzi ordered his commander-in-chief Xinzhi Muzi to attack the City of Zhai. Not only did Zhai fall, but the cities of Zuoren and Zhongren soon after. When he heard the news of these stunning victories, Zhao Xiangzi looked worried. His ministers, puzzled, asked him why he was so glum.

Zhao Xiangzi replied, "Rivers cannot keep rising for more than three days, a storm cannot rage forever, and the sun is high at noon only for a short while. I fear that this quick rising to the zenith will mean an equally rapid decline for our people."

When Confucius heard about this, he said, "The State of Zhao will prosper soon!"

Showing concern and planning things beforehand leads to prosperity, while being carried away by success spells disaster. Keeping victory is more difficult than winning victory. Wise rulers knew this, so they could enjoy happiness and transmitted it to their later generations. The states of Qi, Chu, Wu and Yue had won victories, but they all perished at last, for their rulers did not know how to keep victory. Only he who knew this truth could keep victory.

"On Charms," *Lie Zi*

Note: *Zhao Xiangzi was not happy at hearing the news of unexpected victories, for he knew that keeping victory was more difficult than winning victory. Later sure enough, the State of Zhao flourished day by day, finally becoming one of seven strongest states in the Warring States Period.*

70. Using a Three-Pronged Strategy

The State of Qi once held the crown prince of the State of Chu as a hostage. When King Huai of Chu died, his son asked to be allowed to return home and take his father's throne. The ruler of Qi agreed, but only on condition that Chu surrender 500 square *li* of territory on its eastern border to Qi.

The crown prince thereupon asked to consult his tutor Shen Dao. Permission being granted, he conferred with Shen Dao, who said, "In these extraordinary circumstances I think you may bow to your captor's demand."

This the crown prince did, but after returning to his native state and assuming the throne, he had second thoughts about his promise. Again he consulted Shen Dao. The latter said, "Listen to the words of your officials when they attend court tomorrow morning."

The next day, the first official to speak on the subject, Zi Liang, advised the new ruler to keep faith with Qi, for fear that Chu might lose credibility with its allies otherwise. "After all, Your Majesty, " he argued, "we can take back the lost territory by force of arms at any time it suits us to do so."

The second official to speak, Zhao Chang, urged all-out resistance to Qi's demand. "Apart from the fact that your promise was extracted under duress, Sire, you have to consider that the loss of 500 square *li* would weaken Chu to the point of collapse," he reminded his sovereign.

The third official, Jing Li, was also against surrendering the pledged territory, but he advised forming an alliance with the powerful State of Qin as a guarantee against an invasion by Qi, which would be sure to be angered by a refusal to hand over the parcel of land.

The ruler was at a loss which of the three suggestions to accept, so he consulted Shen Dao again. The latter said, "Follow all three pieces of advice, Sire."

He then went on to explain:

"First, send Zi Liang as an envoy to Qi, who will surrender the land. The very next day, you must appoint Zhao Chang minister of war, with orders to defend the eastern territory. And then, the following day, send Jing Li to Qin to ask for help."

His master was impressed with this plan, and straightaway dispatched Zi Liang to pretend to hand over the land. No sooner had he done so than the newly appointed minister of war, Zhao Chang, sent a large force to defend the eastern territory. When the ruler of Qi questioned Zi Liang as to the meaning of this, the latter replied, "It seems that Zhao Chang is in revolt against the ruler of Chu. Your Majesty should take this opportunity to help the ruler of Chu put down this rebel while at the same time enforcing your will as regards Chu's eastern territory."

So the ruler of Qi sent a large army to march on the eastern territory. But before they got there they were halted by a huge combined force from both Chu and Qin.

Unable to match this show of strength, the Qi's ruler was forced to give up his claim on Chu's eastern territory. Thus, by employing a three-prouged stratagem the State of Chu preserved its territory intact without the loss of a single soldier.

"The Inner Chapters," *Shen Zi*

Note: *When neither military action nor diplomatic guide alone seem adequate to deal with a threatening situation, the best response is often a combination of both.*

71. The Interrogation of Zou Ji

The ruler of the State of Qi, impressed by the counsel of the wandering scholar Zou Ji, appointed him a senior minister.

This annoyed the leading scholars of Qi, five of whom—Chunyu Kun, Shen Dao, Tian Pian, Jie Yu and Huan Yuan—decided to interrogate Zou Ji to find out if he was really as wise as he was reputed to be.

Chunyu Kun put the first question to Zou Ji: "A musical instrument, while you have it secure, is complete and can flourish. If you lose it, everything with it will disappear."

Zou Ji said, "I will cherish your teaching, and put it into practice."

Then Tian Pian said, "Pig grease is what enables an axle to turn. But pig grease cannot be used with a square hole."

Zou Ji said, "Sir, I understand what you mean. Obscurity lurks in the right and left edges and corners. I should pay attention to the right and left sides."

Then it was Huan Yuan's turn: "A fine bow is made of glued wood. But the glue can do nothing about stopping up holes."

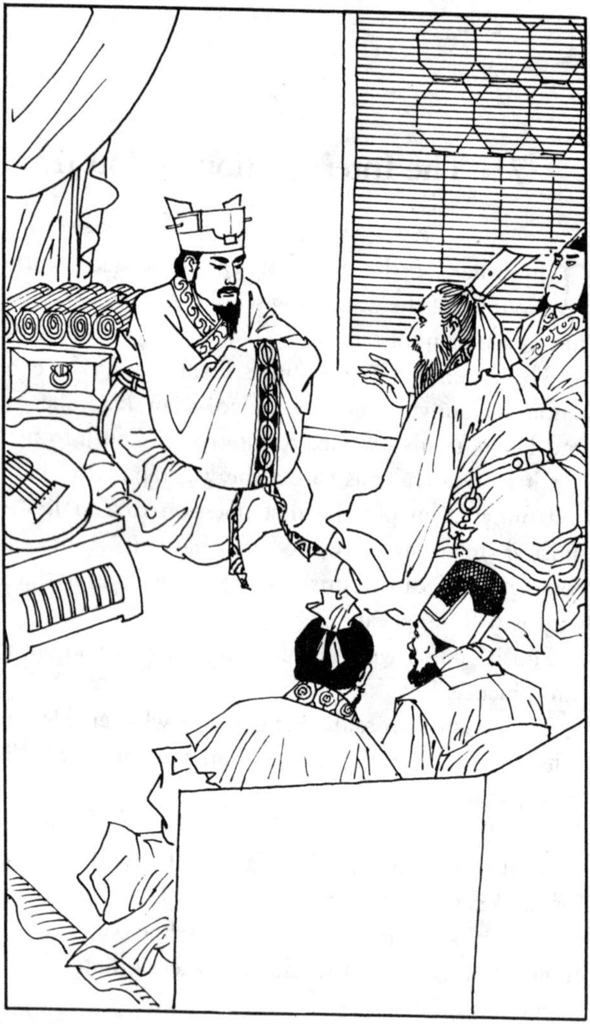

Zou Ji replied, "Sir, I know what you mean. I will encourage freedom of speech and attend to the common people's needs."

Then Jie Yu chimed in, "When a rare fox skin coat is old or ragged, a dog skin or sheep skin coat can not be used, either, can they?"

Zou Ji replied, "Sir, I understand what you mean. I must select talented and virtuous people to assist the ruler and prevent crafty and fawning people from gaining power."

Finally, Shen Dao said, "A big carriage often needs repairing, or it can't carry goods; a fine lute must be often tuned, or it can't play harmonious music."

Zou Ji replied, "Sir, I will do as you recommend, and will reformulate regulations and laws to stop officials engaging in unlawful behavior."

As they left Zou Ji's home, Chunyu Kun said to his colleagues: "Zou Ji is an able man. We asked him five tricky questions, but he was never stumped for a reply. Before long he will be honored with a rank and title of nobility by our master His Majesty."

Sure enough, Zou Ji was made Marquis Cheng of the fief of Pi one year later.

"The Inner Chapters," *Shen Zi*

Note: *In this episode, Zou Ji's agile thinking is held up for admiration, while the questioners' arrogance is mocked. Zou*

Ji gave clear replies to obscure questions, thus revealing his wise and resourceful nature.

72. The Criteria of Talent

The ruler of the State of Qi said to Yin Wen (c. 360-280 B.C.): "I long to employ talented men, but I can not find one anywhere. Can you tell me the reason?"

Yin Wen said, "Sire, may I enquire what kind of people you regard as talented? For instance, a person who is loyal to his ruler, filial to his parents, faithful to his friends and modest in his position--would you consider him talented?"

The ruler said, "Yes, indeed."

Yin Wen said, "If you met such a person, would you appoint him to an official post?"

The ruler said, "I would, but it is not easy to find such a person."

Knowing that the ruler of Qi was a man with a chivalrous and martial spirit, Yin Wen rejoined, "If this person dare not take up arms against an outrageous action in public, would you still want his services?"

The king replied, "A really brave man never hesitates to do what is right, or he will be disgraced. I don't want to use a man who is willing to endure disgrace."

Yin Wen said, "So such a person's timidity would outweigh his four virtues, in your eyes! And that means that you do not consider possession of the four virtues possession of true talent."

When the ruler had no reply to make to this, Yin Wen continued, "If there were a ruler who confused right and wrong, doled out rewards and punishment regardless of merit or blame, and complained that his country was going to rack and ruin because of others' carelessness, would you consider this a feasible way to run his country?"

"No," said the other, "I would not."

"Well, Your Majesty, in my opinion, your country is just like that."

"Oh no!" protested the ruler of Qi. "My officials are not talented; so things are often amiss. It is not as bad as you say. Anyway, what can I do about it?"

"The reason you cannot attract men of talent, Your Majesty, is because your words do not match your deeds and your standards of talent are not consistent. In such circumstances, even a man who had ten times as much talent as the Yellow Emperor could not run the country well."

"Ji Fu," *Gongsun Longzi*

Note: *The author wishes to point out that selection of the talented must be done using consistent standards, and running* *a state demands congruity in speech, thinking and action, that is to say, as Taoism holds, doing nothing which goes against nature.*

73. Three Years of Blame and Three Years of Praise

Yan Ying (?-500 B.C.) inherited the post of senior minister of the State of Qi from his father. During his three years as governor of Ping'a he was slandered by his enemies to duke Zhuang of Qi (reigned 553-548 B.C.). The duke took Yan Ying to task, whereupon the latter admitted that he had been at fault, and asked for another chance.

The duke reluctantly agreed, but during the following three years was delighted to hear nothing but praise about the way Yan Ying was governing Ping'a. He attempted to reward Yan Ying, but the latter balked at this. When asked why, he said, "During my first three years in office, I enforced the law strictly. I was blamed for doing this by Your Majesty. I have just completed another three-year term during which I was neglectful of my duties, and in consequence made no enemies among the rascally local officials. I should be punished, not rewarded."

When Zi Hua Zi heard of this, he said, "Yan Ying is an upright man. His refusal of a reward is a warning to others. At the same time, it is a sign of the decadence of Qi. For every action there is a reaction. If the ruler cannot recognize the action from which a reaction springs, there will be chaos in the administration."

"Bei Gong Zi Shi," *Zi Hua Zi*

Note: *During Yan Ying's first three years in office, he made enemies by governing justly, and so he was slandered. During his later three years in office, he did not offend anybody, and so he was praised. Yan Ying's refusal of a reward proved him an upright man. Only when a ruler bestows praise and blame appropriately can political chaos be avoided.*

74. Qin Shi Mourns for Lao Zi

When Lao Zi died, his friend Qin Shi came to mourn for him. He uttered three yells and went out again. The disciples of Lao Zi asked him, "Wasn't the Master a friend of yours?"

Qin Shi replied, "Certainly."

The disciples then asked, "If so, was it proper to offer your mourning merely in the way you did?"

Qin Shi replied, "Yes. At first, I thought the other mourners were followers of Lao Zi; now I know they are not. When I went in to mourn, there were old persons weeping as if for the loss of their children; and young ones, as if for that of their mother. These persons assembled there uttered words and dropped tears, which are not to be expected. This is to violate the principle of nature and to increase the emotion of man, forgetting what we have received from nature. This was called by the ancients the penalty for violating the principle of nature. When the Master came, it was because he had the occasion to be born. When he went, he simply followed the natural course. Those who are quiet on the proper occasion and follow the natural course cannot be affected by sorrow or joy.

Such people were considered by the ancients as being like the gods, as they had been released from bondage."

The candle may not be able to supply all the fuel. But the flame is transmitted, and we know not when it will come to an end.

"The Fundamentals of the Cultivation of Life," *The Inner Chapters of Zhuang Zi*

Note: *If you are tranquil with the passage of time and follow nature, the things which happen to the body, even death, need not trouble you, and you can combine with Heaven as one. Cultivation is mainly to cultivate the spirit, not the body. The body (candle) may die, but the spirit (flame) will live forever.*

75. Running Water Can't Mirror Things

In the Spring and Autumn Period, in the State of Lu there lived a man called Wang Tai, who had lost a foot. His followers were as numerous as those of Confucius. Chang Ji enquired of Confucius, saying, "Wang Tai is a cripple. Yet he divides with you, sir, the teaching of the State of Lu. He neither preaches, nor discusses. Yet, while those who go to him are empty, those who come back are full. Is there, indeed, such a thing as instruction without words? While the body is deformed, may the mind be perfect? What sort of man is he?"

Confucius replied, "This master is a sage, and the only reason I have not been his disciple is that I was late. I will make him my teacher, to say nothing of those who are not equal to me. I will lead the whole world to follow him, to say nothing of the State of Lu."

Chang Ji asked, "Since his authority is above yours, not to mention ours, Sir, how very different he must be from ordinary people! How exactly does his heart function?"

Confucius replied, "Death and birth are great

considerations, yet neither can affect him. Though Heaven and Earth were to be overturned and to fall, he would remain unmoved. He sees clearly the most perfect and is not affected by lesser things. He knows that the evolution of things is due to destiny, and thus he keeps the essential."

Chang Ji still could not understand, and asked, "What do you mean?"

Confucius said, "If we see things from the point of view of their differences, even liver and gall are as far away from each other as Chu from Yue. If we see things from the point of view of their identity, all things are one. The latter viewpoint is what this man takes. So he knows not even to what his ears and eyes are appropriate, but dallies with the harmony of virtue. He sees the unity of things, but not his own loss. He considers the loss of his foot just as the falling away of so much earth."

Chang Ji thought a while and said, "In the cultivation of himself, with knowledge he attained the mind. With the mind he attained the eternal mind. But why have things gathered around him?"

Confucius said, "Men do not seek to see themselves in running water, but in still water. Only what is still can gather things together. Of those who receive the influence of earth, only the pine and cypress are green both in winter and summer. Of those who received the influence of Heaven, only Shun was correct. Fortunately, he could correct his own life, and then the lives of others. By preservation of the original strength and by elimination of fear, a single brave man may fight his way successfully through nine armies. If such a result can be achieved by this brave man, who can sacrifice himself in search of fame, how much more by one who would control Heaven and Earth and embrace all things, who considers his body as a temporary lodging, and his ears and eyes as mere conveyors of images, who unifies all that knowledge knows, and whose mind never dies. He would choose a day on which he would ascend afar, and people would follow him. How could he care about worldly affairs?"

"Signs of Real Virtue," *The Inner Chapters of Zhuang Zi*

Note: *Wang Tai's authority was above Confucius', for he knew the unchanging Tao and looked at things with the idea of their unity. That was why people followed him. The author wants to say that Taoism is better than Confucianism. The perfection of virtue lies not in the body, but follows nature, ignoring right and wrong, likes and dislikes.*

76. Three Wishes from the Guard of Hua

Once the ancient tribal leader Yao paid a visit to Hua Prefecture. The guard of Hua, having heard that Yao had the virtues of a sage, paid a call on him personally. When they met, he wished for a long life for Yao, but Yao politely declined; then he wished that Yao would be wealthy, but Yao rejected with thanks; at last he wished that Yao would have many sons, but Yao still declined with thanks. The guard enquired, "Long life, wealth and many sons are what most people want. Why do you not want them?"

Yao replied, "Many sons bring many conflicts, worry and fear grow. He who has many sons lives in a constant state of anxiety. Wealth brings many troubles, and long life brings many problems. Beset by worldly things and unable to extricate oneself, one will find one's reputation cannot help but be tarnished. Sir, your three wishes would not enhance the virtues of a sage, but bring troubles, so I eschewed them."

The guard smiled and said, "When I first saw you I thought you were a sage. Now I can see that you are just a nobleman lacking in profound thought. Everything has its own strong points and functions. People are given responsibilities and officials depend on their different abilities. The able get much. What need is there for you to worry and fear? If you share your wealth with others, there will be no trouble! The sage finds his place as a quail settles, or as a fledgling is fed, and as a flying bird leaves no trace of its passage. If the whole world has the Tao, he is part of that well-being. When the whole world has lost the Tao, he develops virtue and avoids involvement. After a thousand years, wearied by the world, he departs and ascends to be with the immortals, soaring upon the white clouds until he arrives at the Supreme One's abode. The three troubles you quote never affect him. They do not touch his body, and such a man suffers no shame!" The guard then turned to leave.

Yao began to realize something and wanted to ask more, but the guard said, "Please leave quickly, since you have understood what I meant."

"Heaven and Earth," *The Outer Chapters of Zhuang Zi*

Note: *The pursuit of long life, wealth and many sons are hindrances to the cultivation of virtue. But regarding these things as burdens is also harmful. In the author's opinion, the ruler should engage in all activities equally, and become a practitioner of the Tao of Heaven.*

77. Called an Ox or a Horse

Shi Cheng Qi had long wanted to meet Lao Zi. When his wish was finally fulfilled, he looked the wise man up and down, saying, "I had heard that you, Sir, were a sage, so I came to see you without regarding a thousand miles as too far. Now I find, Sir, that you are not the sort of person I imaged. I find that you are so wealthy that even the rat holes in your house are full of left-over rice."

Lao Zi showed no emotion and made no reply.

The next day Shi Cheng Qi came to see him again and said, "Yesterday I was rude to you, Sir. Today I have no heart to do so. Why is this?"

Lao Zi said, "You came to see me because I was called a sage, but I think I am by no means a sage. No matter what name you hear, I am still myself. I do not care what others think of me. If some call me an ox, then I would say that I am an ox. If some call me a horse, then I would say I am a horse. If you care that the name matches the reality, but you refuse the name others give to you, trouble will come. So, I never think of a name matching reality, not to mention following the name others give to me."

Shi Cheng Qi felt ashamed. He came forward once more and asked humbly: "Sir, may I cultivate your way?"

Lao Zi said, "Your face is sanctimonious and arrogant; your eyes glare; your forehead is broad; your mouth hangs open; your style is pompous; you are like a tethered horse waiting to bolt. Even if you were forced to cultivate yourself for a moment, you would still be ready to shoot off like an arrow from a crossbow. Furthermore, you examine everything in too much detail; you are cunning in your use of knowledge, and self-willed and conceited. Out on the frontier someone like you would be called a bandit."

"The Tao of Heaven," *The Outer Chapters of Zhuang Zi*

Note: *He who has the Tao of Heaven never cares about skill, right or wrong, praise or blame. Arrogant people cannot attain the Tao, and are harmful in their natures, like bandits.*

78. The Tale of the Skull

On his way to the State of Chu, Zhuang Zi saw a weathered skull lying by the wayside. He prodded it with his riding crop, saying, "Sir, why are you in such a condition? Did you die young because of greedy desire? Were you slaughtered by the barbarians? Did you commit suicide for you were easy in your morals and afraid of bringing disgrace on your family? Or was it perhaps the cold and hunger that reduced you to this? Sir, perhaps it was just your fate, and you died a natural death?"

So saying, he lay down to sleep, using the skull as a head-rest.

At midnight he saw the skull in a dream. It said, "Sir, the things you mentioned today are burdens when people are alive. We dead have nothing to do with this. Would you like to know about life after death?"

"Certainly," said Zhuang Zi. "Be so kind as to tell me."

"People come to our realm after death. The dead have no lord over them, no servants below them. We need not work through the four seasons, so we live freely and will last as long as Heaven and Earth. A monarch on his throne could not be happier."

Zhang Zi could not believe this, and craftily suggested, "If I got the Harmonizer of Destinies to bring you back to life, Sir, with a body, flesh and blood, and let you go back to your hometown to meet your parents, wife, relatives and friends again, wouldn't you like that?"

The skull frowned, and said, "Why should I want to cast away happiness greater than that of kings and become a human being again with all life's burdens?" Then the skull disappeared.

When Zhuang Zi woke up, he saw only shards of the skull. He then continued on his way.

"Perfect Happiness," *The Outer Chapters of Zhuang Zi*

Note: *This fable claims that death is happier than life, for after death people need worry about nothing. This is an extremely pessimistic idea.*

79. Making an Example of a Monkey

The King of Wu (reigned 514-496 B.C.) was sailing on the Yangtze River. He moored his boat in order to climb a mountain known for its monkeys. When the monkeys saw the king and his party, they fled in terror and hid in the bushes. However, there was one monkey who was not afraid, but went on playing, swinging from one tree to another, back and forth, and showing off before the king. The king shot an arrow at it, which the monkey simply caught cleverly in its hand. The king then ordered his followers to shoot a volley of arrows at it, and it soon fell dead.

The king said to his friend Yan Bu Yi,

"That monkey was showing off, relying on its skills, and looked down upon me. That resulted in its death. Men should be warned by this: Do not let yourself seem arrogant to others."

So Yan Bu Yi went home and studied with the hermit of the State of Wu, Dong Wu, to eliminate all traces of arrogance from his face, and to give up contentment and his usual air of eminence. Within three years he was praised by everyone.

"Xu Wugui," *The Miscellaneous Chapters of Zhuang Zi*

Note: *The monkey died because it showed off its skill. So people should not be over-conceited and ignore the existence of others; otherwise, they will meet the same fate.*

80. Gazing at Confucius' Carriage

Once Confucius traveled to the State of Chu with his disciple Zi Lu. Putting up at a tavern on Ant Hill, they noticed that the family next door had clambered on to the roof to gaze at the carriage of the famous visitor.

"What are those people staring at?" wondered Zi Lu.

Confucius said, "They are followers of a sage. He is hidden among the people, hidden away in the fields. He is so great that his voice disappears, but his ambition is big; his mouth speaks words, but his heart offers none. He is not at ease in this dusty world. I imagine he is Xiong Yiliao of Southern Market."

Hearing this, Zi Lu wanted to summon the hermit. But Confucius said, "There is no need to do so. He knows that I comprehend all about him, and he knows I am traveling to Chu. He assumes that I have come to visit him in the name of the ruler of Chu, and thus he views me as a time-server. Someone like him is embarrassed just hearing the words of a time-server, let alone being seen with one. And why do you believe he is still around?"

Half believing, half doubting, Zi Lu went and looked, and found the house empty.

"Ze Yang," *The Miscellaneous Chapters of Zhuang Zi*

Note: *Through Confucius' mouth, the author praised hermits like Xiong Yiliao, who wanted nothing to do with worldly things.*

81. Yang Zhu Asks About His Wrongdoing

The eloquent Yang Zhu traveled south to the State of Pei, while Lao Zi went west to the State of Qin. They did not meet again until they reached Liangcheng (today's Kaifeng). Lao Zi stood in the middle of the road, gazed up to Heaven and said with a sigh: "At first, I thought you could be taught, but now I know you are not the person I imagined you to be."

Yang Zhu said nothing. Together with Lao Zi he went to an inn. Yang Zhu went to fetch water for his teacher to wash with, and a towel and a comb. Removing his shoes outside the door, he crawled across the floor to Lao Zi and said,

"Earlier, Master, I wanted to ask you what you meant, but you were busy and I did not dare to. Now seems an appropriate time, so I would like to ask what I've done wrong."

Lao Zi said, "You are always proud and arrogant. Who would wish to be your friend?"

Even before Lao Zi finished speaking, Yang Zhu felt ashamed and said, "Sir, I know now what I've done wrong."

When he first arrived at the inn, everybody kept out of Yang Zhu's way. But after he had been enlightened by Lao Zi as to his mistakes, Yang Zhu mended his ways and everyone at the inn suddenly became attracted to him.

"Supposed Words," *The Miscellaneous Chapters of Zhuang Zi*

Note: *To learn the Tao, one must start with getting rid of an arrogant attitude.*

82. Cao Shang Gains Carriages

A man called Cao Shang from the State of Song was sent by King Yan of Song (reigned ?-286 B.C.) as an ambassador to the State of Qin. When he left Song he was given several fine carriages by the king so that he could make a fine show. The ruler of Qin was so delighted with his eloquence that he gave him a hundred more carriages. On returning to Song, Cao Shang lost no time showing off his carriages. One day he visited Zhuang Zi wearing a proud, self-satisfied look. He said to him: "I can not bear to live in the poor streets of an impoverished village, make sandals and weave mats, and suffer from hunger. This may be my weak point. By impressing a ruler of ten thousand chariots with my skill I am given a hundred of them, this I enjoy and am good at."

Zhuang Zi said, "Really? But I heard that when the King of Qin falls ill, he always pays much. A doctor who removes a swelling and detoxicates it for him will be rewarded with one carriage. A doctor who licks piles and sucks poison gets five carriages. The lower down the service, the more carriages are given. So, Sir, I assume you must at least have been licking his piles to have been given so many carriages? Leave me alone, Sir, I never associate with mean villains!"

"Lie Yu Kou," *The Miscellaneous Chapters of Zhuang Zi*

Note: *This fable satirizes people who are proud of acquiring wealth and reputation by foul means.*

83. Broken Stone and Smashed Cinnabar

Stone can be broken, but its stiffness can never be changed; cinnabar can be smashed, but its color can never vanish. Stone's stiffness and cinnabar's color are all determined by their characteristics, which can not be changed and chosen by people at will. The integrity of an honest patriot with heroic spirit cannot be stained.

When the Zhou Dynasty rose on the ruins of the Shang Dynasty (c. 11th century B.C.), there were two ministers of the State of Guzhu named Bo Yi and Shu Qi. Thinking that King Wen of Zhou was a worthy ruler, they journeyed west to pay homage to him.

However, soon after they arrived in the Zhou capital, King Wen died, and was succeeded by King Wu. To the great chagrin of Bo Yi and Shu Qi, King Wu was not the sage ruler his predecessor had been, but governed in a worldly way. They lamented, "What a tragedy! This is different from what we had heard and imagined. Long ago, when Emperor Yan ran the country he did nothing going against nature and asked for nothing. The sacrifices in the four seasons were sincere and respectful. He followed the people's wishes, and never sought success by harming others or asserted his superiority by belittling others. But now, King Wu boasts that the Mandate of Heaven destroyed Shang and delivered its people into Zhou's hands. He seems unaware that his actions are the same as those of the degenerate rulers of Shang."

So the pair decided to leave the territory of Zhou and seek enlightened rule in the north. Although they suffered from cold and hunger when they travelled to Mount Shouyang, they refused to eat the foodgrain grown on Zhou soil, and before long they were starved to death.

"Cheng Lian," *Master Lu's Spring and Autumn Annals*

Note: *What Bo Yi and Shu Qi longed for was a peaceful world ruled in a way that did nothing contrary to nature. They steadfastly retained their exemplary conduct and nobility of character. Their spirit of opposing violence and trust in virtue and benevolence were like stone, the stiffness of which can never be changed and cinnabar, the color of which can never vanish.*

84. A Temple Protects a City

Lord Meng Chang of the State of Qi was enfeoffed at the strategic city of Xue. At that time Qi was at loggerheads with the neighboring State of Chu. The ruler of Qi sent Chunyu Kun as an envoy to Chu, and on his way back the latter visited Lord Meng Chang in Xue, where he was hospitably received by the Lord. Chunyu Kun reported to his sovereign that Chu was preparing for war against Qi, starting with an attack on Xue.

"I suppose the worthy Meng Chang is making all preparations to defend Xue," the ruler of Qi said.

Chunyu Kun replied, "When I saw him, Your Majesty, he was constructing an ancestral temple, nothing more. He seemed unconcerned that if Chu attacked the defenseless Xue then the temple would be destroyed."

The ruler of Qi turned pale: "That temple is dedicated to my ancestors!" he thought in alarm. And he immediately dispatched an army to defend Xue.

"Bao Geng," *Master Lu's Spring and Autumn Annals*

Note: *By showing courtesy to the wise,* Meng Chang *was able to ensure the safety of his city. He neither opposed the force of* Chu *with his own force nor did he bring pressure to bear on his ruler. Instead, he accomplished his goal in a way that was completely in accord with nature.*

85. Strong Points Cannot Obscure Weak Points

Strategist Wu Qi asked the senior minister of the State of Wei, Shang Wen: "Are a person's wealth and worldly glory determined by Heaven?"

Shang Wen, puzzled, asked, "What do you mean?"

Wu Qi said, "Protecting border cities and pacifying the border tribes; enacting regulations and educating the common people; breaking with old customs and habits; instilling faith and reason in the ruler and his officials; advocating virtue; and ensuring that the relations between father and son are in order. In all these things, who makes more contributions, you or me?"

Shang Wen replied, "Certainly you."

Wu Qi went on, "Serving the ruler with deference and making his position stable and the state strong. In this aspect, who is better, you or me?"

Shang Wen admitted, "You are above me."

"Soldiers and horses are well arrayed," continued Wu Qi, "and the commanders show exemplary bravery." In this aspect, who is superior, you or me?"

Shang Wen replied, "You are, of course."

"Since I am better than you in the above three aspects," enquired Wu Qi, "how has it come about that you have a higher position than I do? Is this determined by Heaven?"

By way of reply, Shang Wen said, "If a young ruler is unfamiliar with administration, officials distrust each other and the common people live troubled lives, internal security must be given priority. Which of us, do you think, would be the most suited for this task?"

Wu Qi was silent for a while, and then said, "You would."

Shang Wen said, "Since you think so, you must admit that my position should be higher than yours."

Wu Qi, as a talented general, could work out splendid plans to win victories in battles a thousand miles away. But he only thought of his strong points, ignoring his lack of ability to preserve peace at home; he knew only his talents, but knew nothing of virtue and faith. That is why he could win a big victory over the State of Qin, but he was not able to counter his enemy Wang Cuo's plot to drive him into exile and bring about his death.

"Zhi Yi," *Master Lu's Spring and Autumn Annals*

Note: *Only when people understand the relations between strong and weak points can they both save the state and keep themselves out of danger.*

86. Dying for One's Teacher, Friend and Superior

Meng Sheng, the leading Mohist of his time, was a close friend of Lord Yangcheng of the State of Chu. Lord Yangcheng entrusted him with his fiefdom, giving him half of a piece of jade as tally. He said to Meng Sheng, "When you receive the other half, you will also be given instructions as to how to dispose of my lands."

Not long after that, King Dao of Chu died (381 B.C.), and in the struggle for the throne that followed, Yangcheng was forced to flee into exile. The next ruler, King Su, declared Yangcheng's lands forfeit.

When Meng Sheng heard of this, he said to his disciples: "I am duty-bound not to surrender Lord Yangcheng's fiefdom without express instructions from him, accompanied by the other half of the jade tally. However, I cannot defy my sovereign, and so the only thing I can do now is kill myself."

One of his disciples, Xu Ruo by name, protested, saying, "If your death, Sir, were to be in any way beneficial to Lord Yangcheng, it would be your duty to kill yourself. But I am afraid that that is not the case, and the only outcome would be the loss of the leader of the Mohists."

But Meng Sheng disagreed, explaining, "The relationship between Lord Yangcheng and me is a threefold one: teacher-and-pupil, friend-and-friend, and superior-and-inferior. If I do not die, I will be betraying three principles and bringing Mohism into disrepute."

Xu Ruo, realizing that he was in the wrong, thereupon killed himself with his own sword.

Meng Sheng sent two of his disciples to Tian Xiang Zi of the State of Song to ask him to assume the post of leader of the Mohists. Following this, he committed suicide, and his 180 other disciples followed suit. The two who had gone to Song wanted to join them in death, but Tian Xiang Zi forbade it. Nevertheless, the pair made their way back to Chu and killed themselves before Meng Sheng's tomb.

"Shang De," *Master Lu's Spring and Autumn Annals*

Note: *The Great Teacher of Mohism, Meng Sheng, and his disciples died for faith. The Mohists' highest ideal was to be faithful to what others entrusted them to do. The two disciples who disobeyed Tian Xiang Zi, however, are regarded as having acted wrongfully in killing themselves.*

87. A Good Teacher Gives His Clothes to His Pupil

Rong Yi left his native State of Qi for the State of Lu, accompanied by one of his disciples. When they arrived at the capital of Lu it was late at night, and the city gate was locked. So they had to find shelter in a hovel on the outskirts. It being midwinter, the night was freezing cold. Rong Yi said to his disciple: "If one of us gives his clothes to the other, one of us will live and the other die. Now, I am a famous person who deals with lofty matters. It would be a pity for me to die. But you are a nonentity; your death would be of no consequence. So you should give me your clothes."

His disciple said, "It is true that I am a nobody. My virtue is incomplete. Therefore, my clothes would defile a worthy such as yourself, I think."

Thereupon, Rong Yi gave his own clothes to his disciple, and froze to death in the night.

"Chang Li," *Master Lu's Spring and Autumn Annals*

Note: *Rong Yi gave his clothes to his disciple to save the latter's life and died for righteousness. His benevolent heart and devoted spirit can be ascertained from this anecdote.*

88. Rotten Meat and Decayed Bone

Human beings as well as all other things come from Yin and Yang, which in turn spring from nature. Nature itself has waning, shortage and damage, as well as flourishing, fulfilling and assembling. So do human beings and all other things. This is the law of nature. The ancient worthies knew it, so they were never worried by selfish ideas and remained calm.

Understanding people knew that life and death were determined. Such people cared about nothing, and could never be confused.

A warrior of the State of Chu named Ci Fei received a precious sword from Gan Sui of the State of Wuyue. As he was going home by boat, in the middle of the river, two dragons wound themselves round the boat. Ci Fei calmly asked the boatman: "Have you ever seen such a phenomenon before?"

The boatman said, "Never."

Ci Fei took off his outer clothes, brandished his sword and said, "If I jump into the water, the worst that can happen to me is to die and become rotten meat and decayed bone. If I fight the dragons, our lives can be saved, even if I have to forfeit my precious sword."

Ci Fei jumped into the water and slew the dragons. Thereupon, all the passengers in the boat resumed their journey in safety.

Ci Fei's exploit came to the ears of the King of Chu, who forthwith appointed him a senior minister. Confucius himself praised the hero.

"Zhi Fen," *Master Lu's Spring and Autumn Annals*

Note: *Ci Fei was praised for his bravery in the face of danger. Before a brutal enemy, compromise and concessions do not work; in order to protect yourself, you must act resolutely.*

89. The King of Chu Is Whipped

King Wen of Chu (reigned 689-677 B.C.) got a sleuth named Ruhuang and arrows made of bamboo. Then he went hunting in Yunmeng for three months without attending to state affairs. Later he found a beauty named Danji in Zigui and took her into his harem. He stayed with her day and night giving no audience to his ministers for a year. The senior minister Bao Shen was worried and admonished him, saying:

"The late king appointed me to assist Your Majesty after his death. Now Your Majesty has been indulging in pleasure-seeking for months caring nothing about state affairs. According to royal regulations, you should be punished by whipping."

The king said, "I deserve to be punished. But since I'm a king, can I be punished by other ways?"

Bao Shen replied, "I dare not change the late king's order. I would rather displease you than disobey the late king."

Bao Shen took a mat and made the king prostrate on it. Then he took a whip and made as if giving him fifty whippings. He did this twice then asked the king

to punish him for his audacity.

The king was moved and said, "It's all my fault. You are not to blame."

Determined to turn over a new leaf, the king had the dog killed, the arrows destroyed and the beauty sent home. Not long after, he conquered thirty-nine minor states to become one of the overlords at the time.

"Frank Admonitions," *Master Lu's Spring and Autumn Annals*

Note: *By accepting criticisms with a receptive mind and mending his ways, King Wen was able to make the State of Chu strong and himself one of the overlords.*

90. Wu Zixu Crosses the Yangtze

In the Spring and Autumn Period, the senior minister of the State of Wu, Wu Zixu (Wu Yuan, ?-484 B.C.), was originally from the State of Chu. His father had been killed by King Ping of Chu and he had fled into exile. One day he climbed to the summit of the Taihang Mountains and sighed as he gazed on the territory of the State of Zheng,

"Zheng is strategically located and has understanding people, but the ruler is mean, they say. I will not offer my services to him."

Wu Zixu then travelled to the State of Xu, where he had an audience with the ruler. Xu was weak at that time, and feared the wrath of Chu if it harbored Wu Zixu. So the latter once more set off on his travels.

His way was beset with danger, as Chu had offered a huge reward for his capture. But an old boatman saved his life by ferrying him across the Yangtze to safety. Wu Zixu offered him his precious sword as a reward, but the old man refused to accept it.

Taking service in the State of Wu, Wu Zuxu assisted Prince He Lu to gain the throne. By this time he was rich and powerful, but he never forgot the old boatman. He often sent his servants to search for the old man, but they never found him. Wu Zixu, assuming that he was dead, made a habit of praying for his soul before every meal.

"Rare Treasures," *Master Lu's Spring and Autumn Annals*

Note: *The boatman and Wu Zixu form a contrasting yet complementary pair. The former does what is right and scorns reward; the latter is ambitious, yet he never forgets a kindness.*

91. Returning Good for Evil

Song Jiu, a senior minister of the State of Liang, was once the magistrate of a county which bordered on the State of Chu. The two states planted fruit trees along the border line. The fruit in the Liang area was much better than that of Chu, for the people of Liang were more diligent. The county magistrate of the Chu area sent people into the Liang orchards secretly at night to damage the fruit trees. The people of the Liang side discovered this, and demanded that Song Jiu allow them to take revenge.

But Song Jiu replied, "Never! How can you speak so? Hatred is the origin of disaster. It would be far better for you to secretly help them improve their orchards every night."

Then every night the Liang people crossed the border to work in the Chu people's orchards.

At first, the Chu people did not think it strange that their fruit trees were growing well, but later they investigated this unusual phenomenon, and found out that their neighbors had been doing them this unusual favor. They reported it to the local magistrate, who, in turn, reported it to the ruler of Chu. The latter was impressed by Song Jiu's wisdom and benevolence, and straightaway set about improving relations with the ruler of Liang.

There then set in a long period of peace and friendship between the two states, resulting from Song Jiu's wise decision.

It is said that, "failure can be turned into success, disaster can be turned into peace." In the same way, Lao Zi recommended "returning good for evil."

"Accomodationism," *Xing Shu*

Note: *As a result of Song Jiu's spirit of returning good for evil, dissension was avoided and friendship was sealed between the two states of Liang and Chu.*

92. Swallow Humiliation and Bear a Heavy Load

Zhao Jian Zi, a senior official of the State of Jin, chose Zhao Xiang Zi, his concubine's son, as his heir. His steward was shocked by this, and asked him,

"Zhao Xiang Zi is low-born. Why did you choose him as your heir?"

Zhao Jian Zi said, "His is a man of great composure, and can silently endure any disgrace or humiliation for the good of the state."

Several days later, another Jin official, Zhi Bo, attended a banquet with Zhao Xiang Zi. The boorish Zhi Bo got drunk and struck Zhao Xiang Zi, whereupon the other officials who were at the banquet urged Zhao Xiang Zi to kill Zhi Bo.

But Zhao Xiang Zi, as complacent as if nothing had happened, said, "My father made me his heir because he thought I could endure any disgrace or humiliation for the sake of the state. If I were to kill Zhi Bo because of this insignificant slight I would be betraying my father's trust."

Several months later, Zhi Bo raised a rebellion. This time Zhao Xiang Zi stood in the forefront of the resistance and crushed Zhi Bo's forces. Zhi Bo was captured while fleeing, beheaded and his skull made into a wine goblet and presented to Zhao Xiang Zi.

"Taoist Teachings," *Huai Nan Zi*

Note: *Taoists stress being soft outside and strong inside. In shifting circumstances, male and female, soft and hard, honor and shame can change into each other. In order to overcome his enemy, Zhao Xiang Zi bore the insult, but he got his revenge at last. He retreated one small step, but he gained the mastery by striking only after the enemy had attempted his hardest blow.*

93. Extreme Bravery Equals Non-Bravery

One day, Hui Meng discussed talent with King Kang of Song (?-286 B.C.). The king said, "I prefer brave and strong people; I do not like those who always talk about benevolence. What do you think?"

Hui Meng said, "I must tell you one thing: Sometimes brave and strong men are not able to wield the swords they bear in their hands, nor to shoot their arrows even when they are notched to the bowstrings."

The king nodded and said, "Go on."

Hui Meng explained, "The reason why they cannot use their weapons is that they lack the desire for utility and material gain. So, in my humble opinion, if you want hordes of people who can all stab and shoot, you should encourage them to pursue utility and material gain. If every one chased after utility and material gain, that would be much better than having a handful of brave and strong men who can not stab or shoot, would it not, Sire?"

The king nodded. "That's what I want," he said.

Hui Meng went on, "The way to achieve this is to follow the example of Confucius and Mo Zi. With not even the tiniest of territories to rule, they have the Tao. Enjoying no official rank, they are universally respected. Now, you are the ruler of a mighty state. If you carry out the Tao, the whole country will benefit. It will be much easier than it was for Confucius and Mo Zi."

Hui Meng then left. The king said to his ministers: "Hui Meng's experience is wider than mine. According to Lao Zi, if he who is brave dare not act, he may live. But if he who is brave dare act, he must die. From this, we can conclude that extreme bravery equals non-bravery."

"Taoist Teachings," *Huai Nan Zi*

Note: *In Hui Meng's opinion, brave people who have no desire for benefits have no spirit to stab or shoot. In the case of such people, their extreme bravery equals non-bravery. When they regard virtue as the most important thing, all people can receive comfort and benefits.*

94. Three Rewards for Three Mercies

During the reign of Duke Jing of Song (516-469 B.C.), a fiery star appeared in the sky. Sometimes it emerged in the west, sometimes in the east, but always above the borders of Song. The duke was puzzled and worried. He consulted Zi Wei, the court astrologer.

"Why is the 'fire star' above our territory?" he asked.

Zi Wei said, "This is a sign from Heaven. It portends that disaster will come upon you. However, you need not worry, for disaster can be shifted. You can transfer it to the prime minister."

The duke said, "No, I can not do that. I need the prime minister to run the country. If I shift this disaster onto him, it will be harmful to the country."

Zi Wei then suggested, "How about shifting the disaster to the common people?"

"If all the common people died I would have nobody to rule. I would rather die myself," the duke objected.

"Then perhaps the disaster can be shifted to the weather," Zi Wei persisted.

But the duke was obstinate: "The weather dictates

the farming seasons. Shifting the disaster to the weather would be tantamount to shifting it to the common people themselves. No, I must bear Heaven's judgment, as I am the head of the state."

A few days later Zi Wei requested an audience with the duke. Entering the court, he said, "Congratulations, Sire! Heaven, which sees all men's deeds and knows all men's hearts, has decided to bestow three rewards upon you for the three mercies you extended to the prime minister, the common people and the weather, respectively. In short, tonight the fire star will move away for the distance of three *she*, and that means that Your Majesty will enjoy another 21 years of life."

He explained that it took a star seven years to move from one *she*, or position in the zodiac, to another. So, by removing the "fire star" three *she* Heaven was warding off the pending disaster by 21 years.

At Zi Wei's suggestion, the duke accompanied him to the roof of the palace, where they did indeed observe the "fire star" moving away for a distance of three *she*.

"Taoist Teachings," *Huai Nan Zi*

Note: *It is in accordance with the teachings of Lao Zi that a person in a position of authority should take upon his own shoulders the sufferings of his underlings. Duke Jing of Song was an exemplary ruler in this respect.*

95. Honor Among Thieves

There was a notorious bandit named Zhi in the late years of the Spring and Autumn Period. One of his henchmen once asked him, "Is there any code of conduct for robbers?"

Zhi said, "The Tao is everywhere. How can even robbers live without the Tao? When treasures are stored in a storehouse, the robber who can come up with the right idea for coming into possession of them, giving sage advice to his fellows, is regarded as a genius by the other robbers; he who cooperates with his fellows and is not afraid of injuries from defenders is considered to be a brave man among the other robbers; when discovered, he who fights for his fellows without caring about his own life, is regarded as a faithful man among the other robbers; when dividing up the loot, he who takes less is regarded as a benevolent man among the other robbers; he who can analyze the situation and win whenever he takes action, is regarded as a wise man among the other robbers. Without these five virtues, how could I be a great robber? In fact, just as a good man must exhibit the five virtues if he wishes to be esteemed in good society, so must a robber exercise the five virtues if he wishes to be esteemed in the fraternity of the gentlemen of the highway."

"Taoist Teachings," *Huai Nan Zi*

Note: *It is one of the ironies of life that both the sage and the robber share the Tao.*

96. Good Deeds Will Be Vindicated

A man of the State of Song devoted himself to doing good, a trait which he had inherited from his grandfather. One day his black cow bore a white calf. He consulted a fortune teller about this, and was told that it was an auspicious sign and that the calf should be offered as a sacrifice to the gods. The man did do, but instead of being blessed with luck disaster struck when his father was stricken blind. At the same time, his black cow bore another white calf. His father advised him to sacrifice this one to the gods, too, despite his son's protests that the sacrifice of the previous one had brought calamity and not good fortune.

This time too, disaster struck, as the son went blind. Not only that, but the State of Chu invaded Song and besieged its capital. When the capital fell, the Chu troops massacred the defenders and enslaved all the able-bodied men. But the father and son escaped both fates, being blind.

Before long, both of them miraculously recovered their sight, rebuilt their home and resumed their work of doing good.

"Lessons from the Human World," *Huai Nan Zi*

Note: *Three generations of good deeds accumulated blessings for the father and son, although in a way that they did not expect.*

97. Unfair in Meting Out Rewards and Punishments

The three states of Wei, Zhao and Han together attacked the State of Qi and encircled Ping'a, a city of Qi. The minister Kuo Zi said to the senior minister Niu Zi:

"The three states of Wei, Zhao and Han are not contiguous to Qi and Ping'a is not a place of abundance either. In coming from so far off to attack Ping'a they seek obviously not for material gains, but rather for flaunting their strength to intimidate the other states. You had better request His Majesty to go to Ping'a in person to deal with the matter."

Niu Zi thought it reasonable, but another official, Wu Hai Zi, objected, saying: "There are many ways to relieve a state of its crisis, like ceding the country's land to satisfy the other country's territorial claims, sacrificing one's life to save his country from destruction, and so on and so forth. I have never heard about a monarch going in person to a troubled place to deal with the matter."

As the decision maker, Niu Zi accepted Kuo Zi's suggestion instead of Wu Hai Zi's empty talk. As a result, the states of Wei, Zhao and Han withdrew their troops and Ping'a was saved. After that, the king of Qi, however, promoted Wu Hai Zi to a higher official post and estranged himself from Kuo Zi.

The king of Qi was criticized by later generations for being unfair to Kuo Zi, who had the national interest at heart, and partial to Wu Hai Zi, who tried to curry favor with the king at the expense of the state's interest.

"Lessons from the Human World," *Huai Nan Zi*

Note: *The king of Qi's unfairness in meting out rewards and punishments showed that he was not a good monarch.*

98. Biding One's Time

In the Warring States Period (475-221 B.C.), there was a crafty and fawning official at the court of the ruler of the State of Chu named An Lingchan. He was sturdy and handsome and was the ruler's favorite. One of his friends, named Jiang Yi, visited him and asked, "Did any of your ancestors distinguish himself in battle for Chu?"

"No." replied An Lingchan.

"Did you yourself ever distinguish yourself in battle for Chu?"

"No."

"Why are you loved by the king?"

"I do not know either."

Jiang Yi said, "I have heard that friendship that relies on money will end when the money runs out; love will vanish when beauty changes. Now you are young and beautiful, but when you become old, how will you retain the ruler's favor?"

An Lingchan said, "Please give me your advice."

Jiang Yi said, "You can ask him to allow you to be buried with him."

An Lingchan said, "I'll follow your teaching."

One year later, Jiang Yi met An Lingchan and asked him: "Have you asked our sovereign about what I advised you one year ago?"

An Lingchan said, "Not yet."

Another year went by, and again Jiang Yi asked An Lingchan: "Have you mentioned that matter to the ruler?"

An Lingchan said, "I have had no chance as yet."

Jiang Yi was puzzled. He said, "But you have been attending his court for three years. Moreover, You share his carriage regularly. That at any rate should give you an opportunity for a quiet word in his ear. However, if you hesitate to accept my advice there is nothing I can do."

One day the ruler went hunting together with An Lingchan. The hunting was very successful, and the ruler was happy. He turned to An Lingchan, and said, "Today we are both happy. If I die, who will you be happy with?" Thereupon, the favorite seized his chance and pleaded, "Your Majesty, allow me to be buried alongside you. How could I ever be happy with another?"

This delighted the other, and he responded by granting An Lingchan a city of 300 households on the spot.

"Tactics and Strategies," *Garden of Anecdotes*

Note: *Planning and strategy are necessary to achieve one's ends, even if one is a fawner and flatterer.*

99. The Skillful Robber

A man surnamed Guo in the State of Qi was very rich. A man surnamed Xiang in the State of Song was very poor. Xiang went to Qi to ask Guo how to become rich.

Guo told him, "I'm skillful at robbery. After I started to steal, I had no need to worry about food or clothes in the first year, became rich in the second year and waxed prosperous in the third year. I share my prosperity with my neighbors."

Xiang was very happy to hear this. He thereupon went back to Song and immediately started to clamber over walls and steal everything he could lay his hands on. Before long, however, he was arrested, and his ill-gotten gains were confiscated. Xiang thought Guo had cheated him, so he went back to Qi to blame Guo.

Guo asked him, "How did you rob?" Xiang told him.

Guo shook his head sadly. "I see that you don't know the real meaning of robbery," he said. "Heaven has four seasons and Earth has rich resources. I steal favorable climatic and geographical conditions. Clouds and rain can irrigate, mountains and rivers can cultivate. I rob them for planting grains and building houses. I rob beasts and birds on the land, fish, shrimps and tortoises in the water. Everything comes from robbery. Grain, earth, timber, beasts and fish are all products of nature. Which one belongs to me? But my robbery can not bring any disaster. Treasures, grains and money, all make others prosperous. Aren't they given by Heaven?"

Hearing this, Xiang was even more confused. He went to consult a wise man called Dongguo.

Dongguo said, "Doesn't every part of the human body come from robbery? Stolen Yin, Yang and *qi* make up your life and body, not to mention the things outside your body. Everything is stolen. Certainly, everything is related. You regard them as your own, for your heart has been confused. Guo's robbery accords with the public benefit, as it brings no disaster; yours is private desire, so you committed crimes. Both, however, are robbery. Both public and private are the virtue of Heaven and Earth. If you really know the virtue of Heaven and Earth, who cares whether you are a robber or not?"

"Tian Rui," *Lie Zi*

Note: *This fable tells us that we must really understand what others mean and must not take action blindly. In Lie Zi's opinion, the definition of robbery is unlimited, even* *including a human being's production activities using natural resources. Taoism holds that everything in the nature is one and cares nothing about right and wrong.*

100. An Old Farmer Explains the Tao

Zi Hua was the favorite of the ruler of the State of Jin. Although he had no official position, he enjoyed wealth and power. His influence over the ruler was such that one word from him was enough to ruin a man or set him up for life. His mansion was thronged with attendants and flatterers.

One day two of Zi Hua's hangers-on took a pleasure trip into the suburbs. As night came on, they put up at the hovel of a farmer named Shang Qiukai. Late into the night Shang eavesdropped as his guests talked admiringly of Zi Hua's prestige and power. The poor farmer then decided to seek the patronage of Zi Hua.

When the fops and dandies who loafed around Zi Hua's mansion saw Shang Qiukai in his peasant rags requesting admittance to the exalted presence of Zi Hua they roared with laughter. Then they started to play all kinds of cruel tricks on the country bumpkin.

One day they took him to the edge of a precipitous cliff. Some one said, "Whoever dares to jump from this cliff will receive 100 pieces of gold." Everyone pretended to scramble to be the first to jump, but hung back at the last minute, while the simpleton Shang Qiukai launched himself over the edge. To the astonishment of the others, Shang floated like a bird and came to rest on the ground below utterly unharmed.

Thinking that this must have been some accidental stroke of luck on Shang's part, they next took him to a deep river. Pointing to the deepest spot, one said, "There are treasures down there; the first to reach them can keep them." Shang Qiukai unhesitatingly dived in and swam to the bottom. Not long after, he emerged with an armful of precious objects.

When he learned of these feats, Zi Hua treated Shang Qiukai with the greatest respect.

One day, the storehouse where Zi Hua kept his silks caught fire. The frantic Zi Hua offered a huge reward to anyone who could save his precious silks.

Thereupon, Shang Qiukai dashed into the burning storehouse and rescued the silk goods, making several sorties and always unscathed by the fire.

By this time Zi Hua and his clients realized that Shang Qiukai was a man who had mastered the Tao. They asked him how he had acquired this wonderful secret. Shang Qiukai protested that there was no secret: "I believe your words and put my utmost trust in you," he said. "Serene in mind, I put aside all thoughts of my body. That was how I managed to survive a tremendous fall, deep water and raging fire. But now that I know that you were deceiving me all along, I am cautious about my body and do not dare approach danger."

"The Yellow Emperor," *Lie Zi*

Note: *This fable stresses that he who has sincerity and concentration can overcome any difficulty. Whatever we do, we must have determination, confidence and perseverance. But it is also important to study actual conditions and understand the objective laws.*

101. Master and Servant Have Opposite Dreams

There was once a rich man who worked his servants very hard. One old servant found his duties most exhausting, but every night he used to dream that he was the king of the country, presiding at banquets and honored far and wide. Whenever somebody sympathized with him for his hard life he would say, "Although I spend half my life in cruel toil, I spend the other in joy and ease. Why should I complain?"

His master, on the other hand, while enjoying riches and fame during the day, every night dreamed that he was somebody else's servant. His dreams were a torment of backbreaking labor and hard blows. He consulted a friend about his uneasy nights, and the friend said, "Your dreams accord with the universal order of things. Pain and happiness change into each other in due degree. It is impossible to be either constantly happy or constantly miserable."

Hearing this, the rich man decided to make life easier for his servants. As a result, his nights became less burdensome, as did his old servant's days.

"King Mu of Zhou," *Lie Zi*

Note: *Pain and joy alternate. Only restraint of one's desires can ensure moderation of these two opposites.*

102. The Three Doctors

The eminent Taoist Yang Zhu had a friend named Ji Liang. One day Ji Liang fell ill. As his condition became worse, his sons asked Ji Liang to let them call a doctor.

Ji Liang said to Yang Zhu: "My sons do not understand that it is useless to consult physicians in this case. Please enlighten them."

Yang Zhu said, "If Heaven does not know, how can man know? Good fortune is not determined by Heaven, and disaster is not caused by man. You and I can not know. How can doctors and soothsayers know?"

Ji Liang's sons did not understand what Yang Zhu meant, and so they scurried around looking for doctors here and there. They found three, surnamed Jiao, Yu and Lu.

Doctor Jiao said to Ji Liang: "Your heat and cold are not balanced, and deficiency and excess are not limited. Your disease is caused by hunger, avarice and carnal desire. This is determined by neither Heaven nor evil spirits. Although you are seriously ill, you still can be cured by medicine."

Ji Liang burst out with "See this charlatan off the premises!"

Doctor Yu said, "You were born weak. It is impossible to cure your illness, for it was formed over a long period of time."

Ji Liang said to his sons: "This is a fine doctor. Let him stay for dinner."

Doctor Lu said, "Your disease is not determined by Heaven, man or evil spirits. When people receive life from Heaven, there is someone mastering and knowing it. How can medicine do anything about your ailment?"

Hearing this, Ji Liang could not help exclaiming, "This is a magical doctor. You must present him with precious gifts!"

Not long after, Ji Liang made a complete recovery.

"Li Ming," *Lie Zi*

Note: *Doctor Lu confirmed what Ji Liang already knew: only by letting nature take its course can one find ease. This is the proper way as taught by the Tao.*

103. No Mourning for a Son

There was a man named Wu in the State of Wei. He refused to mourn when his son died. His steward could not help asking him: "Sir, you loved your son very much. Why are you not sad now that he has died?"

Wu said, "Before I had a son, I was not worried. Now that he has died, the situation is just like before. Why should I mourn?"

"Li Ming," *Lie Zi*

Note: *This is what Taoists would call a natural attitude to life and death.*

104. The Way of Life and Death

Yang Zhu said, "An ancient saying goes, 'People should love each other when they live, abandon each other when they die.' This is wise advice. Loving each other means easing the burden of the toiler, feeding the hungry man, giving the cold man warmth, and succoring poor man. Abandoning each other does not mean feeling no sorrow when others die. It means burying the dead without costly funerary objects or monuments.

Yan Zi (?-500 B.C.) asked the former statesman Guan Zhong about the way of life. Guan Zhong said, "The way of life is to let oneself be. Never restrain your any desires."

Yan Zi asked, "Would you mind telling me in detail?"

Guan Zhong replied, "Listen to what your ears want to listen to, see what your eyes want to see, smell what your nose want to smell, say what your mouth wants to say, go wherever your body wants to go. In a word, you should do whatever you want to do. The ears want to listen to sounds. If they are not permitted to do so they will become dull. The eyes want to see beauty. If they are not permitted to see it their brightness will dim. The nose wants to smell fragrance. If it is not permitted to do so the sense of smell will be blocked. The mouth wants to speak right and wrong. If it is not permitted to do so one's wisdom will be blocked. The body wants to be comfortable. If this is not permitted, happiness and comfort will cease. People wish to have their own way. If they are not permitted to have their own way their natures will be blocked. All these blocks are the main things that harm people's bodies and hearts. Living a peaceful and happy life without these blocks is my way of life. If you cannot get rid of the blocks, then even if you were to live 1,000 years you would never be free from care. That is not my way of life."

Guan Zhong then asked Yan Zi, "I've told you my way of life. Can you tell me your way of death?"

Yan Zi said, "Dead people can be put into water, buried, thrown into the wilderness, covered with grass, or dressed in official robes and placed in stone coffins. Let the living deal with them as they will."

Guan Zhong turned to his friends Bao Shuya and Huang Zi, and said, "It seems that Yan Zi and I know both the way of life and the way of death."

"Yang Zhu," *Lie Zi*

Note: *Guan Zhong and Yan Zi reject self-cultivation and treat death and life as matters of indifference.*

105. He Who Can Run Quickly Does Not Run Slowly

Yang Zhu had an audience with the ruler of the State of Liang. He told the monarch: "Running a country is as easy as waving your hands."

The other said, "Sir, you can not deal with your wife and one concubine and three *mu* of land. Why do you say that running a country is easy?"

Yang Zhu replied, "Sire, a small child can control a flock of more than 100 sheep with only a whip. But, if you make the sage emperor Yao lead a sheep and another sage emperor, Shun, follow behind with a whip, the sheep may not go forward at all. And I also heard that the big fish which can swallow boats never swims in small rivers; the large swan which can fly high never comes to rest on a muddy pool. Why? It is because they have ambitious goals. He who can run quickly does not run slowly, he who can achieve a big success does not stop at a small one."

"Yang Zhu," *Lie Zi*

Note: *Big and small are comparative terms; there is no impassable gulf between them. As different stages of the development of things, cultivating the self, running a family, a country, or even the whole world are first related and then different. It is reasonable that he who can deal with big things can not handle small ones. But, it is absurd to say that he who can achieve a big success may not achieve a small one.*

106. A Hungry Man Refuses Rice

Lie Zi lived in the State of Zheng. At one time he and his family fell upon hard times and had to go hungry. Somebody brought this to the attention of Zi Yang, the prime minister. Zi Yang thereupon sent a quantity of rice to Lie Zi. The latter, however, refused to accept it.

When Lie Zi's wife heard about this she scolded her husband roundly.

Unfazed, Lie Zi explained, "Zi Yang does not really appreciate me. He must have heard from others about my plight, and so sent me the rice. In the future, he may hear slander from others concerning me. That is why I did not accept his rice."

Later, the people of Zheng rebelled and killed Zi Yang, but Lie Zi, being known to have snubbed Zi Yang over the matter of the rice, escaped their wrath.

"Shuo Fu," *Lie Zi*

Note: *This anecdote testifies to Lie Zi's wisdom and foresight. He gave up a small advantage and preserved his life.*

107. The Pen and the Sword

The Shi family of the State of Lu had two sons. One loved the pen, the other loved the sword. The son who loved the pen went to the State of Qi, where he was appointed tutor to the sons of the ruler. The son who loved the sword went to the State of Chu and was made an officer of the Chu army for his martial arts skills. The two sons' salaries made the Shis rich and all their relatives and friends were proud of them.

The Shis' neighbor, surnamed Meng, also had two sons, who had acquired, respectively, the same as the Shis' two sons. But they were poor. The Mengs' sons asked the Shis' sons how they had managed to become so wealthy.

The Meng youths then decided to try to reproduce the Shi young men's success.

One of the Mengs, who was skilled in administration, went to the State of Qin. The ruler of Qin said to him:

"Nowadays, all states are fighting for power, only soldiers and supplies are useful. If you use benevolence to run my state, that will lead to disaster."

The ruler then had Meng tortured to punish him

for his temerity, and then sent him home.

The other son of the Mengs, who was skilled in martial affairs, went to the State of Wei. The ruler of Wei said to him: "As a weak state, Wei is under pressure to appease the major states. Diplomacy is what we need. If we rely on martial virtue, we'll be lost. Although I cannot employ you, if I let you go, you may take your martial prowess to another state and use it against us."

Thereupon, he had the young man's feet cut off before sending him home.

Having met with nothing but misfortune by following the Shis' advice, the Mengs blamed their neighbors.

But the Shis merely protested, "It is all a matter of timing. What you learned yesterday may be useless today, but useful tomorrow. There is no fixed standard for what is useful and what is useless. The essence of wisdom is the ability to identify and seize opportunities."

The Mengs recognized that this was indeed so. Thereupon, they resigned themselves to their poverty-stricken fate.

"Shuo Fu," *Lie Zi*

Note: *This fable stresses that dogmatism and empiricism are disastrous trends of thought, for everything changes due to condition, location and time. The situations in Qi, Chu, Qin* *and Wei were different, so the people they needed were necessarily different. From this story, we can gain profound enlightenment: Whatever we do, we must act according to circumstances; following old patterns must lead to failure.*

108. The Tooth and the Tongue

The grandson of Confucius, Zi Si, was appointed prime minister by Duke Mu of Lu. Before taking up his post, he visited the hermit Lao Lai Zi. Lao Lai Zi asked him,

"Now, you're going to assist the ruler. What do you plan to do?"

Zi Si said, "I'll follow my own disposition as well as my sovereign's wishes. That way, I am sure that nothing will go wrong."

The hermit shook his head. "If you follow the inclinations of your personality," he said, "I am afraid you will come to grief. You are too stiff and severe by nature. I counsel you to learn to be more compliant. Take a tooth, for example. It is hard, stiff and unyielding. But eventually it decays, breaks and falls out of the mouth. The tongue, on the other hand, is soft and yielding; it can never be destroyed."

"Kang Zhi," *Kong Zhong Zi*

Note: *Lao Lai Zi advised Zi Si to be like the tongue*

—pliable—in his official life, and not follow the inclinations of his personality, which was inclined to be stiff and unbending.

109. A Fraudulent Gift

A farmer of the State of Wei one day found a lump of pure jade in one of his fields. Not knowing what it was, he consulted his neighbor. The latter was a rascal who recognized that it was a precious material, but deceived the farmer by saying, "I see nothing but evil coming of this strange stone. You had better put it back where you found it."

The farmer was unsure what to do, so he took the piece of jade home. As night fell, the jade started to glow in the dark. The farmer and his family were frightened by this, and the next morning the farmer told his neighbor about this strange phenomenon. The neighbor said, "That is proof that it is an evil stone. Get rid of it at once!"

The farmer thereupon threw the jade away in a field. The crafty neighbor, however, had carefully noted where it landed, and as soon as the farmer left, he picked up the jade and presented it to the ruler of Wei. The ruler summoned a jade expert to inspect the piece, and the master craftsman pronounced it flawless and invaluable. The neighbor was rewarded with 1,000 pieces of gold and a lifetime's salary equal to that of a senior minister.

Everything under Heaven is either right or wrong. But the right may not find its proper time, and may become usurped by the wrong.

"Da Dao Shang," *Yin Wen Zi*

Note: *This story tells how the honest farmer was cheated by his sly neighbor. The latter prospered because the good did not find its proper time, and was usurped by the bad.*

110. Touching the Tiger's Forehead

In 279 B.C. Lin Xiangru foiled the ruler of the State of Qin's plot at the meeting between Qin and Zhao at Mianchi, and was appointed prime minister of Zhao as a reward. Under his stewardship, the State of Zhao was stable and peaceful.

Once, meeting Shen Zi, Lin Xiangru boasted, "People all think that Qin is as strong as a tiger. Well, I've touched this tiger's forehead and tapped its shoulder. I am not afraid of it."

Shen Zi said, "Well, sir, you indeed showed courage on that occasion. But I heard that there was a stone bridge between high cliffs in the mountains of Chicheng. Smooth as jade, the bridge was one *chi* in width, had no railing and was arched like a tortoise's back. It spanned a bottomless chasm. Once a man living in the mountains strode nonchalantly across this bridge carrying a bundle of faggots. The people who saw him do it all gasped in admiration.

"But as soon as someone praised him for his courage, the man looked down into the chasm, and was so overcome with fear that he fell a-trembling and never dared try to cross the bridge again.

"You, sir, are like this man. When you dared to 'touch the tiger's forehead' you were unaware of how dangerous the ruler of Qin is. But now, after serving as prime minister of Zhao for some time, you know full well how fierce he can be. I do not think you will dare touch any part of that particular 'tiger' again."

"The Outer Chapters," *Shen Zi*

Note: *Lin Xiangru did indeed show courage during his confrontation with the ruler of Qin. But he was not as wise as Shen Zi, who was able to see past the appearance to the reality.*

111. One Hundred Questions for Divination

A man named Hong Da was kind, generous, faithful, modest and amiable. But one question continually vexed him: If everything under Heaven is one, why are there differences among things? He could not understand that the truth was buried beneath the surfaces of things and appearances were only the work of form. Then one day he consulted the diviner Taishi Zhenfu.

Taishi Zhenfu arranged the tools of his trade —yarrow stalks and a tortoise shell—and asked, "What can I do for you?"

Hong Da said, "Should I openly speak blunt words at the court or follow others? Should I be amiable and upright or chase after interest and fame, following others blindly? Should I do good secretly or smooth over my faults? Should I be upright or cynical? Should I be like a dragon in deep water or a wild goose flying freely? Should I be indifferent and apathetic or fervent and excited? Should I store treasures, eat rare food, wear beautiful clothing and surround myself with beauties or live in distant mountains, drink from rivers and rest on stones? Should I act like Lao Zi, doing nothing and pondering the inner mystery, or like Zhuang Zi, knowing everything and forgetting himself? Should I ignore small shame and assist the ruler, like Guan Zhong, or ignore interest and fame, like Lu Zhonglian? ...... Sir, can you tell me, which is gain, which is loss, which is good and which is bad?"

Taishi Zhenfu said, "I have heard that a true man never visits fortune-tellers and a worthy one never requests divination. Sir, you have virtues inside you and know the ways of both ancient and modern times. You can travel all over the land free of cares. Why do you worry about the inner reality of the world?"

Hong Da had no reply to make to this.

"Consulting the Oracle," *Collections of Ji Kang*

Note: *Taishi Zhenfu could not clear up Hong Da's doubts. It is unnecessary for a man who has virtues inside himself and knows the ways of both ancient and modern times to worry about the inner reality of the world. At the same time, it is impossible to resolve doubts by divination.*

图书在版编目(CIP)数据

中国道家故事选:英文/元光编. —北京:
外文出版社,1999
ISBN 7-119-02163-X

Ⅰ.中… Ⅱ.元… Ⅲ.故事-作品集-中国-当代-英文 Ⅳ.I247.8

中国版本图书馆 CIP 数据核字(1999)第 03589 号

责任编辑 吴灿飞
英文编辑 程 宇
封面设计 王 志
插图绘制 李士伋

外文出版社网页:
http://www.flp.com.cn
外文出版社电子邮件地址:
info@flp.com.cn
sales@flp.com.cn

中国道家故事选
元光 编
*

外文出版社出版
(中国北京百万庄大街 24 号)
邮政编码 100037
北京外文印刷厂印刷
中国国际图书贸易总公司发行
(中国北京车公庄西路 35 号)
北京邮政信箱第 399 号 邮政编码 100044
1999 年(36 开)第 1 版
1999 年第 1 版第 1 次印刷
(英)
ISBN 7-119-02163-X/I·497(外)
03500(平)
10-E-3258P